COLLINS
ATLAS OF
EXPLORATION

DINAH STARKEY

CONTENTS

INTRODUCTION

This book is about the great explorers of the world. It tells the story of their journeys and adventures.

We know something about these journeys because the travellers left evidence behind them. In the very early days, before people could read and write, that evidence might be a map or a picture, a carving, a sculpture or a story passed down through the years.

Later explorers kept a log of their voyage – a sort of diary which described their journey, day by day. Some wrote about their adventures after they came back. More recent expeditions often included an artist or a photographer, who could bring back pictures.

All these kinds of evidence help us to find out about the journeys of exploration that took place from different countries at different times.

However, we don't know so much about the people whom the explorers met. We say Columbus 'discovered' America. That sounds as if the land was empty until he got there. Of course, this is not true. The islands of the Bahamas were a new and strange country to Columbus and his crew, but to the people who lived there, they were home. This book also tells the story of the native peoples – the ones who got there first.

3

HOW THE MAPS WORK

Most of the pages in this book feature a large map showing the routes taken by the explorers. On each of these maps you will find:

A compass to show the direction taken by the explorers and the relation of one place to another.

A scale to show the distances covered by the explorers and the relative distance between one place and another.

0   200   400   600 kms

A key to the map to show the routes taken by individual explorers. Where an explorer has made more than one journey, the dates of his different journeys are given.

> **KEY TO MAP**
> ~~~~~~~ Park 1795~96
> ‒ ‒ ‒ ‒ Park 1805~6
> ········· Caillié

Sometimes you will see that a place has been given two names, eg:

Molucca Islands
(Spice Islands)

This happens when a place that is now known by the first name shown (Molucca Islands), was known at the point of history in question by the second name shown (Spice Islands).

Sometimes you will see that a place has been given only a name in brackets, eg:

(Babylon)

This happens when a place existed at the point of history in question, but now no longer exists.

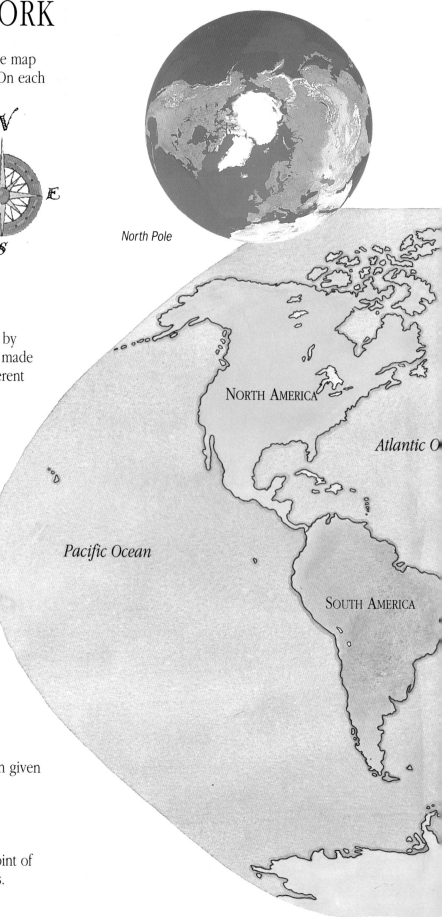

North Pole

NORTH AMERICA

Atlantic O

Pacific Ocean

SOUTH AMERICA

WORLD MAP

Below is a map showing the continents and oceans of the world. This is for your reference when following the explorers' routes shown inside this book. The maps with the explorers' routes show only the part of the world that the explorers travelled. By referring to this world map, you can see the relative distance covered by the explorers and the location in the world of their journeys.

It should be noted that different map projections are used throughout the book, depending on the area being illustrated. For example, a map of the Antarctic, such as the one found on pages 54-55, shows the area of the Antarctic as seen from above (see also the aerial view of the South Pole on this page). Both are accurate views of Antarctica. However, when the Antarctic is shown using a different projection, as it is in the world map on this page, you can see that it appears quite different, both in its shape and area.

Arctic Ocean

ASIA

EUROPE

Pacific Ocean

AFRICA

Indian Ocean

AUSTRALASIA

Southern Ocean

ANTARCTICA

South Pole

5

THE EXPLORERS OF THE ANCIENT WORLD

England

MEDITERRANEA

AFRIC

THE EGYPTIANS

Who was the first person to go exploring? We don't know. We do, however, know the first one to be named: he was called Harkhuf and he lived in Egypt.

Over 4,000 years ago, the king of Egypt sent Harkhuf further into Africa to look for rare woods and treasure. He travelled overland, taking with him a great train of camels and donkeys, known together as a 'caravan'. It took Harkhuf's caravan several months to reach the area now known as the Sudan, in the north of Africa.

As well as ivory, ebony and fur, Harkhuf brought back a dwarf dancer, who may have been a member of one of the African Pygmy tribes.

Nearly 800 years later, Queen Hatshepsut of Egypt

sent sailors to the Land of Punt, which was probably in modern-day Sudan or Somalia. The Egyptians took presents for the king and queen of Punt. When they returned to Egypt, their ships were laden with cinnamon wood and ebony, gold and ivory, monkeys, panther skins and 31 young frankincense trees, each one in its own pot.

KEY TO MAP
```
-------  Harkhuf
———————  Hatshepsut
— — — —  Phoenician voyages
```

0   200   400   600 kms

FRANKINCENSE TREES
When burning, the resin of the frankincense tree gives off a sweet smell. It was used by the Egyptians in their temples to please the gods.

6

KEY DATES
- **2270 BC** Harkhuf's expedition set out
- **1700–1450 BC** Minoan civilisation at its height
- **1493 BC** Queen Hatshepsut sent her expedition to Punt
- **1100–300 BC** Phoenicians traded throughout the Mediterranean region

TYRIAN PURPLE

Tyrian purple was a dye. Only the Phoenicians knew the secret of how to make it. The dye was made from sea shells. It was a wonderful purple colour. Cloth dyed this colour was so beautiful and so expensive that only kings and emperors were allowed to wear it.

AFTER THE EGYPTIANS

THE BABYLONIANS

In southwest Asia the Babylonians studied the sky and tried to solve the mystery of what was beyond the Earth. They decided that the Earth was round and that it was encircled by sea. They thought there were islands in the sea, which made stepping stones to heaven. The Babylonians were the first people to name the four points of the compass.

THE MINOANS

The Minoans of Crete traded throughout the Mediterranean. They made pottery decorated with spirals and sea creatures. People are still finding bits of it today.

THE PHOENICIANS

The Phoenicians lived in northwest Syria. They were brilliant sailors, trading in cedar wood, glass and Tyrian purple dye.

The Phoenicians sailed to a place called Ophir, which was probably situated somewhere on the southwest coast of Arabia, on a mission for King Solomon. As well as cedar wood, they brought back gold and silver, ivory, apes and peacocks.

They sailed all over the Mediterranean, down the coast of Africa and even further. Some people think they came all the way to England to buy tin, but we can't be sure because the Phoenicians never wrote anything down. They kept their routes secret for fear other people would use them and they're still unknown to this day.

BLACK SEA

ASIA

Syria

Crete

Tyre

(Byblos)

(Babylon)

Egypt

The Sudan

Nile

RED SEA

(Arabia)

(The Land of Punt)

BABYLONIAN MAP

This is one of the oldest maps of the world. It was made in Babylon in the 7th century BC.

7

THE GREEKS

The people of Ancient Greece lived about 2,000 years later than the Egyptians and Babylonians. They were interested in all kinds of learning and several of them went on to become the first true scientists.

In the 4th century BC, a Greek called Aristotle proved that the world was round. He noticed that the line where the sky met the Earth (the horizon) was very slightly curved. He showed that it was curved because the world was round.

It was the Ancient Greeks who made the first proper maps. Egyptian and Babylonian maps were not very accurate; the people who drew them invented the parts they didn't know, because they didn't believe that accuracy mattered. But the Greeks tried hard to find out more about the world so that they could draw better maps. When a sailor returned from foreign lands, he would tell the map-makers about everything he had seen and they would draw it carefully. If they couldn't find out any information about an area, they left it blank to show that they knew nothing about it. They didn't make anything up.

Greek maps were better than any which had existed in the world before. They were also better than many that came later. In fact they were so good that when Columbus set off to look for the Indies in 1492, he took with him a copy of a Greek map that was more than 1,000 years old. After all that time, it was still the best he could find. It was called the Ptolemy map because it had been drawn by a Greek named Ptolemy.

LATITUDE AND LONGITUDE

The Greeks invented new ways of showing the world clearly. A Greek called Eratosthenes was the first to draw lines of latitude and longitude on a map. These are imaginary lines, still used by map-makers to divide up the world. Lines of latitude go across the world; lines of longitude go from top to bottom. The equator is a line of latitude.

ALEXANDER THE GREAT

In 334 BC Alexander the Great took a whole army exploring. Alexander was king of Greece and he planned to conquer the neighbouring empire of Persia. He led his army into Egypt, where he founded a city, which he named Alexandria. He travelled further and further to the east over the huge mountains of the Hindu Kush until his army reached the wide River Indus.

Alexander ordered his men to build a bridge of boats, and in this way they crossed the river. Alexander wanted to advance further east, but his men were tired of travelling and they refused to go any further. With his army, Alexander sailed down the River Indus to find out where it led to, aiming to return to Greece by sea. They reached Susa in the Persian Gulf in 324 BC, but Alexander never got home to Greece. He died, possibly of malaria, at the age of 32.

PYTHEAS

One of the greatest Greek explorers was Pytheas of Massilia (Marseilles). He sailed along the west coast of France and all the way round Britain. He sailed north of Britain for six days until he came to a land known as Thule. It was a sunless place where people lived on millet, herbs, berries and fruits. He sailed on until he came to a place where the sea froze over and there were glaciers and volcanoes. We think he may have reached Norway or Iceland, but the book in which he wrote of his journeys has been lost and no one can be certain.

KEY DATES
- **384-322 BC** Aristotle lived
- **334 BC** Alexander led his army from Greece
- ***330 BC** Pytheas sailed from Marseilles to Thule
- ***276-194 BC** Eratosthenes lived
- ***2nd century AD** Ptolemy lived

*exact date unknown

THE VIKINGS

The Vikings came from Denmark, Norway and Sweden. These are countries with little good farming land, surrounded by a great deal of sea. So the Vikings made their living from the sea: from fishing, piracy and trading with other countries. They went as far as Russia, trading in amber, furs and whale oil and they were always on the look-out for new land where they could settle and farm. They were great explorers.

They were also excellent sailors and knew how to find their way across the open sea without using land-marks. They used the Sun and stars to help them.

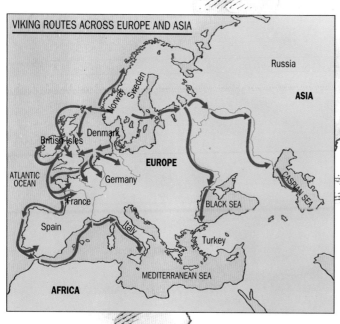

When a Norwegian called Floki Vilgerdasson set sail from Norway in 860 AD to look for new land, he took with him three ravens to help him find the way because he knew these birds can sense when land is near. He let the first one go and it flew back to Norway. Later, he let the second one go and it flew round then settled on the ship. But when at last he released the third one, it flew ahead of the ship. Floki knew it must have found land, so he followed it and soon sighted Iceland.

VIKING ROUTES ACROSS EUROPE AND ASIA

Russia

ASIA

Norway

Sweden

British Isles

Denmark

EUROPE

ATLANTIC OCEAN

Germany

France

CASPIAN SEA

Spain

Italy

BLACK SEA

Turkey

MEDITERRANEAN SEA

AFRICA

KEY TO MAP
— Floki Vilgerdasson
–·– Eric the Red
····· Leif Ericson

Baffin Island

Greenland

NORTH AMERICA (Vinland)

ATLANTIC OCEAN

KEY DATES
- **860 AD** Floki Vilgerdasson sailed to Iceland
- **981 AD** Eric the Red sailed to Greenland
- **1000 AD** Leif Ericson landed in Vinland

VIKING SHIPS

When the Vikings went raiding, they used long narrow ships (longships) to creep up rivers and take their enemies by surprise. When they set off to look for new lands, they took a different kind of ship called a *knorr*. This was bigger and broader than a longship and it was clinker-built. This means that the planks overlapped, which stopped water from leaking in and made the ships stronger. Knorrs were strong enough to stand up to the fierce weather of the Atlantic and they could hold a lot. The Viking explorers took women servants, seeds, cattle, pigs and sheep, all packed into the same boat. The knorrs were not covered over and these long journeys were cold, miserable and dangerous.

VIKING SAGAS

The Vikings liked to make up long tales about their brave deeds. These tales are called *sagas* and some of them tell of the adventures of the Viking explorers. They were great boasters so we can't be sure that the sagas were absolutely true, but we can still learn a good deal from them. One saga tells of an adventurer called Eric the Red. He lived in Iceland, but he had to leave in a hurry because he had killed someone. He was sent away for three years and in 981 AD he went sailing to look for a new land. He found a country which seemed rich and fertile. The sea was full of fish. He called this new country Greenland and settled there with his family.

Eric had a son called Leif. The Viking stories call him Leif the Lucky because, they say, he found a new land. He was sailing near Greenland in the year 1000 AD when his ship ran into storms. It was swept westward until Leif and his crew made landfall on a strange shore. They found fields of wild wheat and grapevines, so they called the new country Vinland. We think Vinland was North America.

Another story names a trader called Bjarni Herjulfsson as the first person to sight America. Whatever the truth of these sagas, it seems likely that the Vikings did reach the American continent long before Columbus.

Left: Eric the Red in Greenland

THE MIDDLE AGES

The map shown here was made 900 years ago. By this time, the fine maps of the Ancient Greeks had been lost. Most people believed that the world was flat and that if you sailed too far away from land, you would meet terrible monsters, darkness and danger.

People in Europe thought Africa was a land of mystery. They heard tales about dog-headed men, cannibals and magical fountains. Somewhere far inland, they believed, was a kingdom which was Christian, with a king called Prester John. People also believed in a river of gold and thought travellers on it might find the Garden of Eden, surrounded by a wall of fire.

People of the Middle Ages had forgotten the skills of earlier times. No longer did sailors dare to cross the open sea. Their ships were not as easy to handle as the Viking boats. So travel was a slow and dangerous business. Most people stayed at home.

Those in Europe who did travel were the traders, who crossed the countries of Europe; pilgrims made their way to Spain and Jerusalem; and knights went on crusade to the Holy Land to fight the Arabs who had taken Jerusalem. Here they had their first taste of the many spices from the Far East which had come via the Silk Route.

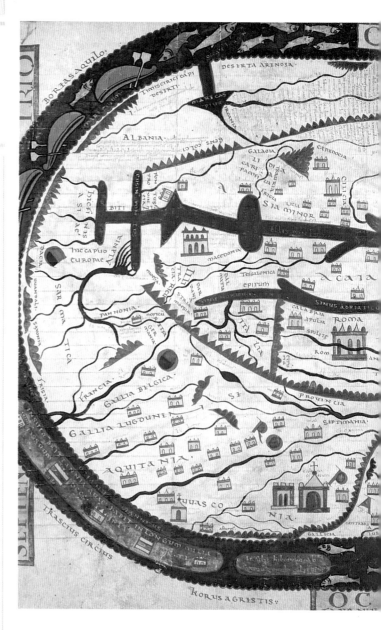

GENGHIS KHAN

In 1206 a new emperor was crowned. He was Genghis Khan, ruler of the Mongols. These people were nomads who travelled the great plain of Mongolia, a vast region of central Asia, with their herds of cattle. They were fine horsemen and fierce fighters. Genghis Khan built up a huge army which swept through Asia, capturing vast areas of land. By 1215, they had reached Beijing in China. When the Khan died, the Mongol Empire stretched from the Yellow Sea to the Caspian Sea. His sons and grandsons went on to invade Russia, Poland and Hungary.

VENICE AND GENOA

Venice (shown left) and Genoa, at the end of the Silk Route, were busy ports. Ships from these ports brought rich goods from the Far East to Italy, France, England and Spain. As a result, the cities became very wealthy – Venice was Europe's richest city in the 13th century.

Map labels

ASIA
EUROPE
Poland
Russia
Mongolia
Venice
Hungary
Genoa
Turkestan
BLACK SEA
CASPIAN SEA
Samarkand
Anxi
Great Wall of China
MEDITERRANEAN SEA
Baghdad
Kashi (Kashgar)
Beijing (Peking)
Iran
Tibet
Xi'an
Korea
Japan
AFRICA
India
China
YELLOW SEA
Arabia
PACIFIC OCEAN

KEY TO MAP
— Silk Route
☐ Mongol Empire in 1260

INDIAN OCEAN
Molucca Islands

THE SILK ROUTE

The Silk Route consisted of several different roads leading from China, where silk was first made over 4,500 years ago, to the Middle East (in the western part of Asia) and Europe. Merchants used it for trading goods such as silk, porcelain, gold and ivory.

13

MARCO POLO

It was 1298 and two men were in prison. To pass the time, one started telling the other tales of his life. He told of elephants and jewels, magicians and fire-eaters, and of a land rich and powerful beyond imagining. The prisoner's name was Marco Polo and he was describing his 17 years in China, at the court of the great Kublai Khan (grandson of Genghis Khan).

Marco Polo was born in Venice in 1254. At the age of about 17, he set out with his father and uncle along the Silk Route to the Mongolian capital of Shang-tu. The journey, which lasted more than three years, took them over huge mountains and across wide deserts to the great Khan's summer palace at Shang-tu. Polo became a servant of the Khan. He travelled all over the Mongol Empire, taking note of everything he saw. On his return, he was captured by the Genoese, who were at war with the people of Venice. His fellow prisoner, Rustichello, wrote down Polo's stories in a book known as *The Book of Marvels*.

THE IMPORTANCE OF MARCO POLO

Marco Polo told of gold and silver, diamonds, rubies and pearls. He described the spices which grew in Java: nutmeg, cloves, peppers and many others besides. He made Kublai Khan's empire sound like a treasure house.

People began to think hard about ways of getting to the Far East because they believed that, once there, they could make their fortune. Christopher Columbus was one of the explorers who read Marco Polo's book and dreamed of finding a way to Java and the Spice Islands.

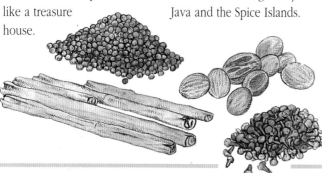

KUBLAI KHAN'S EMPIRE

According to Marco Polo's book, the walls of the Khan's palace were covered with silver and gold. It glittered from afar like a crystal.

In the winter Kublai Khan and his court went hunting. The Khan rode on an elephant in a pavilion covered with lion skins and a cloth of gold. He hunted with hawks and with leopards. Huge numbers of animals were killed.

IBN BATTUTA

Ibn Battuta was born in Morocco in 1304. He was on a pilgrimage to Mecca when he had a dream. He dreamt that he was riding on the back of a great bird which carried him far away into the East. He believed this meant that he must travel east as far as he could. So began a life of journeying from North Africa to China, in which Ibn Battuta encountered thieves and shipwreck, plague and storms. Sometimes he was greeted by kings and showered with gifts. Once he was captured by bandits and threatened with death. Of all the Muslim travellers, Ibn Battuta was the greatest.

TRAVELLING IN THE KHAN'S EMPIRE

The Khan gave orders for good roads to be built throughout his empire. These were planted with plenty of trees to provide shade in the summer. The Khan's messengers, who were chosen for their swiftness, travelled these roads with bells hanging from them so that everyone could hear them coming.

The most important of the Khan's servants carried with them a gold tablet. This was a sign to show people that the Khan's servants could go wherever they pleased and that people must supply them with fresh horses, food, shelter and any other help they needed. Marco Polo, his father and his uncle carried one of these gold tablets with them whenever they travelled.

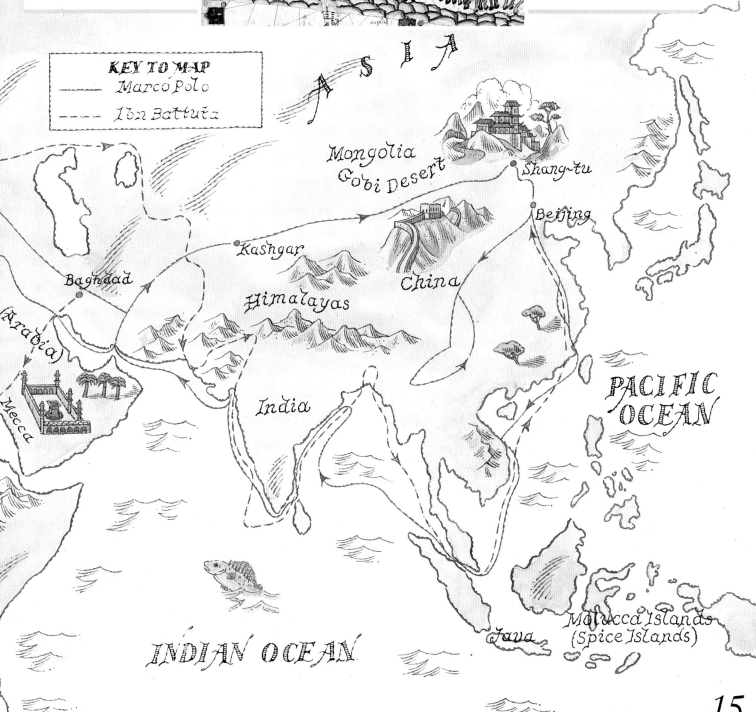

KEY TO MAP
—— Marco Polo
-- -- Ibn Battuta

ASIA

Mongolia
Gobi Desert

Shang-tu

Beijing

Kashgar

China

Himalayas

Baghdad

(Arabia)

Mecca

India

PACIFIC OCEAN

INDIAN OCEAN

Java

Molucca Islands
(Spice Islands)

INTEREST IN THE FAR EAST

Ever since the time of the Crusades in the Middle Ages, rich people in Europe had been buying silks and spices from the Far East. These people were willing to pay high prices for them. Traders knew that as long as they could travel between Europe and the Far East, they could run a profitable business. By the 15th century, though, parts of the Silk Route had been blocked off. The Route ran through Turkey and Arabia, and the people who lived here, the Saracens, were enemies to all Christians. They barred the road and fought off any Christian trader who tried to pass.

By 1450, European sailors had learnt how to use a compass to steer a course. They no longer needed to stay close to the coast all the time. Ships were improving; they were becoming faster and easier to handle. Some ships used the lateen sail, which enabled them to sail against the wind by zigzagging ('beating'). This is sometimes also known as 'sailing close to the wind'.

Marco Polo's book (shown left) told people about the riches of the Far East. Then, in 1410, another important book appeared: Ptolemy's *Guide to Geography* had been lost and forgotten for 1,300 years in Europe. Now a copy was found and translated. The Saracens had blocked the overland route to the Far East, but Ptolemy's map showed that it might be possible to find a sea route to the Spice Islands via Africa. The great age of exploration had begun.

LATEEN SAILS

Early ships used square sails. They only worked well with the wind right behind them. But the lateen sail was triangular and if needed, it could be set to catch a less favourable wind.

EUROPE

Venice

Genoa

Turkey

AFRICA

Nile

RED SEA

Mecc

JUNKS

Cheng Ho's ships were called junks. They were enormous and some carried as many as five sails. The Chinese still use junks today.

CHENG HO (ALSO KNOWN AS ZHENG HE)

While the merchants of Europe were looking for a sea route to India and the Far East, the admiral Cheng Ho set out from China to travel west. He took with him a huge fleet which included 62 treasure ships and 250 smaller vessels. He made seven journeys across the China Sea and the Indian Ocean visiting 30 countries and gathering information about them. His fleet carried up to 30,000 people, including doctors, translators, merchants, craftsmen and priests. The ships stayed at sea for months at a time. On his seventh voyage, his ships sailed a huge distance of 20,307 kilometres.

The Chinese knew more about keeping healthy at sea than the Europeans did. Cheng Ho's crew grew fresh vegetables on board and doctors looked after the sick. Nevertheless the journeys were full of hazards and many people did not survive them.

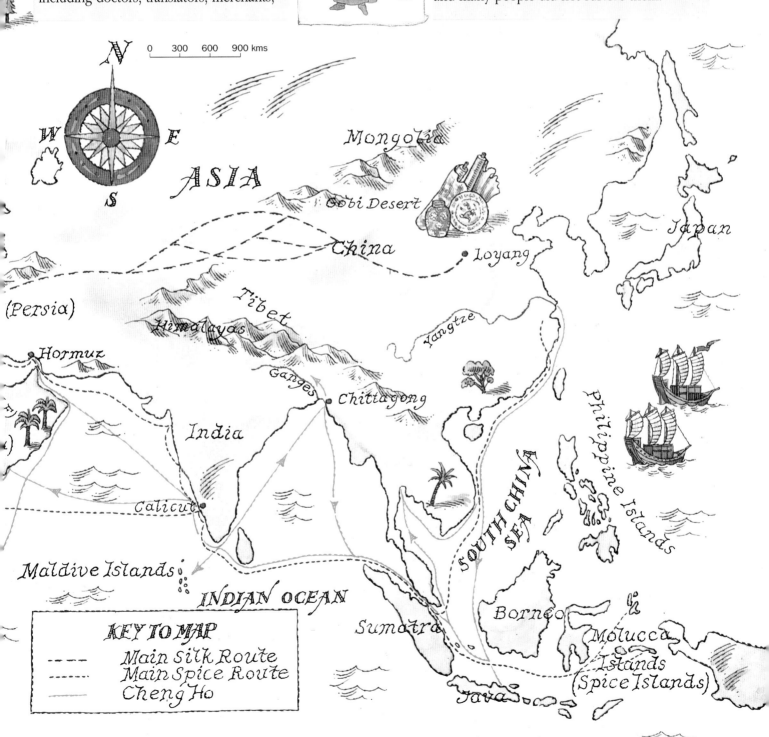

ASIA

Mongolia

Gobi Desert

China

Loyang

Japan

(Persia)

Tibet

Himalayas

Hormuz

Ganges

Chittagong

Yangtze

India

Calicut

Philippine Islands

SOUTH CHINA SEA

Maldive Islands

INDIAN OCEAN

Borneo

Sumatra

Molucca Islands (Spice Islands)

Java

KEY TO MAP
- - - - Main Silk Route
- - - - Main Spice Route
——— Cheng Ho

0   300   600   900 kms

VASCO DA GAMA

Vasco da Gama was a Portuguese explorer born around 1460. This was the year of the death of Prince Henry of Portugal (shown below), who was also

known as Henry the Navigator because of his keen interest in exploration.

In 1433 Prince Henry sent a ship from Portugal to sail down the west coast of Africa as far as possible then come back and report what had been discovered. It was all part of his drive to find a sea route to the Spice Islands.

For 15 years he had been gathering together map-makers, sea captains, geographers, ship builders and every kind of expert he could think of to help him in the project. He offered them land and gold to persuade them to help him. While the experts thought up new ship designs and ways of navigating, Prince Henry's sea captains put them into practice.

The first ships didn't go very far. Sailors believed that beyond Cape Bojador lay the Sea of Darkness, and they were afraid to go on. The ship sent by Prince Henry in 1433 was the first to get past Cape Bojador. Despite Henry's death, the Portuguese continued their voyages of exploration. By 1497, Portuguese ships had reached the southernmost tip of Africa. Under Vasco da Gama the greatest of the Portuguese voyages was about to begin.

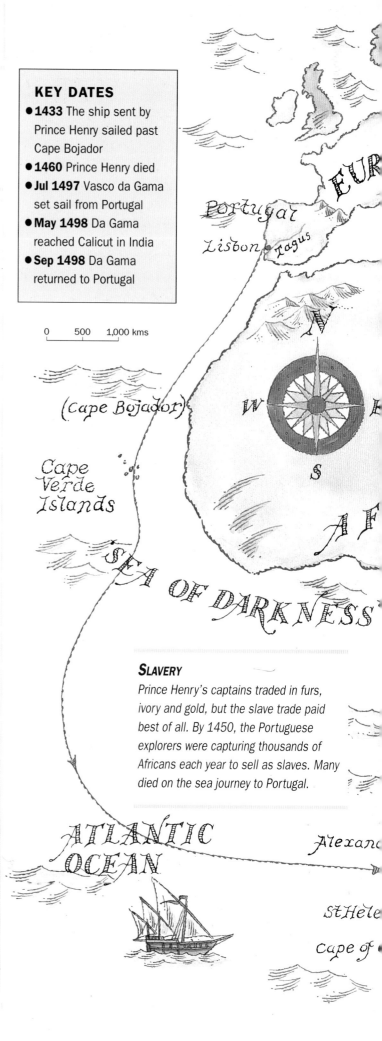

KEY DATES
- **1433** The ship sent by Prince Henry sailed past Cape Bojador
- **1460** Prince Henry died
- **Jul 1497** Vasco da Gama set sail from Portugal
- **May 1498** Da Gama reached Calicut in India
- **Sep 1498** Da Gama returned to Portugal

0   500   1,000 kms

Portugal
Lisbon *Tagus*

EUR

(Cape Bojador)

Cape Verde Islands

SEA OF DARKNESS

A F

W N E S

SLAVERY
Prince Henry's captains traded in furs, ivory and gold, but the slave trade paid best of all. By 1450, the Portuguese explorers were capturing thousands of Africans each year to sell as slaves. Many died on the sea journey to Portugal.

ATLANTIC OCEAN

Alexand

St Hele

cape of

18

THE JOURNEY

On 8th July 1497, Vasco da Gama set sail from the River Tagus in Portugal. He steered for the Cape Verde Islands and then straight out to sea in a wide sweep which, for two months, took the crew far out of sight of land. At last, on 7th November, they sighted St Helena Bay. The crew ran up flags, fired off guns and dressed in their best to celebrate.

It took another two months to round the Cape of Good Hope and sail up the coast of East Africa. On 25th January, da Gama had his first glimpse of the great Arab *dhows* sailing across the Indian Ocean, laden with gold, silver, cloves, peppers, ginger, pearls and rubies.

At Malindi, da Gama picked up an Indian pilot, Ibn Majid, to help them steer the correct course, and on 20th May they reached the Indian port of Calicut. Calicut was very rich; the Arabs who traded there brought fine silks with them and gave its ruler, the samorin, wonderful presents. Vasco da Gama had few gifts to offer and what he had didn't please the samorin. The people of Calicut didn't want to trade with the Portuguese. Da Gama managed to buy some pepper and cinnamon and set off for home. They had a hard journey with bad weather all the way. They got back to Portugal in September to a hero's welcome: Vasco da Gama had found the sea route to India.

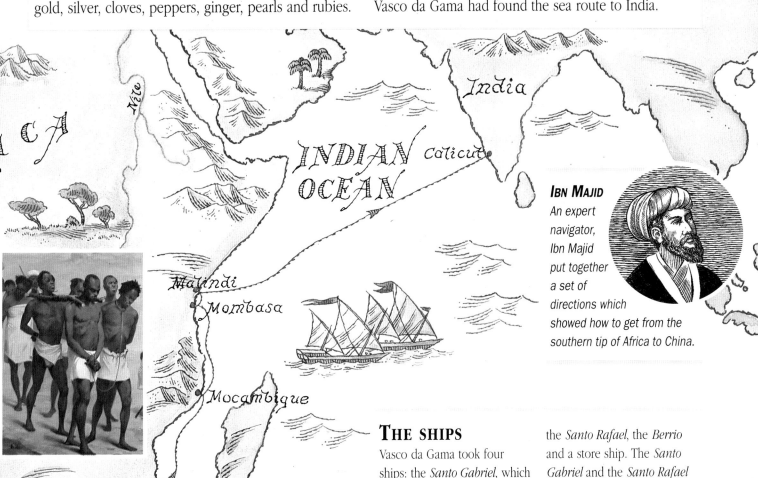

IBN MAJID

An expert navigator, Ibn Majid put together a set of directions which showed how to get from the southern tip of Africa to China.

THE SHIPS

Vasco da Gama took four ships: the *Santo Gabriel*, which was the flagship, the *Santo Rafael*, the *Berrio* and a store ship. The *Santo Gabriel* and the *Santo Rafael* were purpose-built for the long ocean voyage. The *Berrio* was a new *caravel* – a tall, fast ship with lateen sails for sailing against the wind. On board the ships were 170 men and enough supplies to last the crew for three years.

19

CHRISTOPHER COLUMBUS

The port of Genoa in Italy was an exciting place for adventurers in the late 15th century. In the harbour sailors from as far away as Africa and Iceland swapped stories of the sea. A young Genoese boy called Christopher Columbus listened. The stories made him want to sail the oceans, and his seafaring adventures began at the age of 14. These journeys, and conversations with his mapmaker brother, gave Columbus the idea for a grand voyage. He believed he could reach the Far East by going west across the Atlantic Ocean. Columbus hoped to bring back precious silks and spices by sailing on this new route.

Such a daring expedition was very costly, and it was many years before Columbus found someone who would pay for the trip. Eventually, though, King Ferdinand and Queen Isabella of Spain agreed to provide the ships, sailors and supplies that he needed. So in 1492 Columbus was able to set sail from the Spanish port of Palos.

THE NORTH ATLANTIC WINDS

Columbus was able to cross the North Atlantic because he understood the Ocean's winds. In the north, the winds blow from west to east, but further south, they blow the opposite way, from east to west. So Columbus kept to the south on his outward journey and returned to Spain by a northern route.

LANDFALL

On 12th October 1492, after sailing for 33 days, the ships arrived at a small island in the Bahamas. We cannot be sure exactly which island it was, although we think it is San Salvador. The natives' name for this island was Guanahaní. The islanders were curious and friendly. They came out to meet the ships in canoes made of tree trunks. Columbus and the Spanish sailors went ashore carrying the Spanish banner and the admiral's flag, and they claimed the island for Spain.

THE NATIVE PEOPLE

The native inhabitants of the islands discovered by Columbus were generous and peace-loving people. They were happy to share their food and possessions with the strange arrivals to their shores. However, the sailors began to be greedy: they seized cotton, cinnamon and precious stones; later, they took prisoners from among the islanders to sell as slaves.

The islanders caught diseases like smallpox from the Spaniards, which killed them in large numbers. Fifty years after Columbus' expedition first set sail, Hispaniola's native population of about 250,000 had all died out.

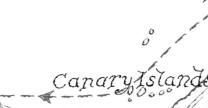

Scale: 0 300 600 900 kms

What they took

Columbus' expedition had three ships which carried enough supplies for a whole year. They took:

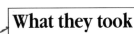
BARRELS OF FRESH WATER

JARS OF OIL

SALT

FLOUR

SALTED MEATS

NETS

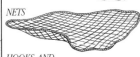
HOOKS AND FISHING LINES

WOOD FOR FUEL

SACKING TO SLEEP ON

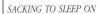

BEADS AND RED WOOLLEN CAPS FOR TRADING

ROUTE TO THE INDIES?

Columbus wanted to be the first person to find a western sea route from Europe to the Indies (the name given to Southeast Asia, India and Indochina). Like other Europeans at that time, he did not know that the continent of America lay in the way. When he landed on one of the islands in the Bahamas, he was sure that he had in fact reached somewhere in the Indies. It wasn't until much later that he discovered his mistake. This is the reason why he called the inhabitants of the island 'Indians', and why the islands off the east coast of America are known today as 'the West Indies'.

21

LIFE ON BOARD

The sailors on board Columbus' ships spent much of their time, both night and day, up in the rigging, adjusting the sails to make the ships travel as fast as possible.

They cooked their food on deck in large pots heated by a wood fire. Only one hot meal was served each day, and that was at 11 o'clock, when the men on watch came off duty to be replaced by a new group of men.

The crew squatted on deck to eat, drinking broth from bowls and picking out the meat and fish with their fingers. They also ate rough bread with their meals. When not working, sailors sometimes fished from the ship's deck. Fresh fish for lunch was considered a treat.

The captain of the ship slept in a cabin, but the sailors slept on deck on rough sacks wherever they could find a spot.

THE SANTA MARIA

Columbus was captain of the *Santa Maria*, the biggest of the ships. In it he crossed the Atlantic from the Canary Islands in a little more than a month. This was a fast crossing, and the crew arrived in the Bahamas not only alive, but fit and well. Modern replicas (working copies) of the ship have never been as fast as the *Santa Maria*.

THE SHIPS

Columbus took three ships on his journey west: the *Niña*, the *Pinta* and the *Santa Maria*. All three ships were caravels – tall-sided sailing ships with three masts, that first appeared in the 15th century. The *Niña* was fast and agile with triangular (or lateen) sails, good for sailing against the wind; the *Pinta* was larger and square-sailed. These sails were better for sailing with the wind.

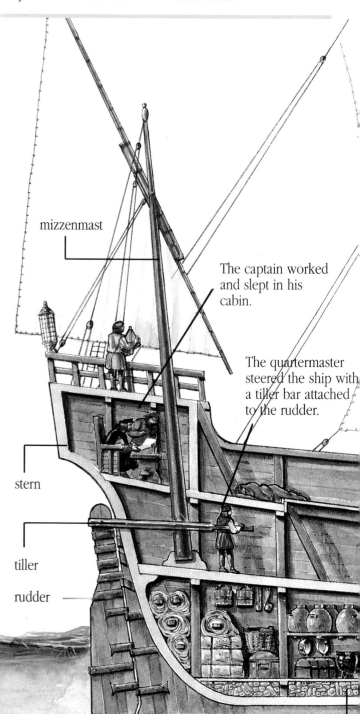

mizzenmast

The captain worked and slept in his cabin.

The quartermaster steered the ship with a tiller bar attached to the rudder.

stern

tiller

rudder

Ballast was used to keep the ship stable.

INSTRUMENTS FOR NAVIGATION

Columbus used simple instruments to help him navigate across the Atlantic. Direction was measured with a compass situated on deck.

Pincers were used for marking off each day's journey on a map. An astrolabe could be used to help show the ship's location by measuring the position in the sky of the Sun and stars.

What they brought back

The islanders gave Columbus and his men gifts of:

PARROTS

COTTON THREAD

PUMPKINS

INDIAN CORN (MAIZE)

DARTS

PINEAPPLES

The sailors also found strange animals:

IGUANAS

GIANT RODENTS CALLED HUTIAS

EXOTIC FISH

The crew quickly copied the islanders' hammocks for sleeping on board ship.

The *Santa Maria* could carry about 100 tons. Her crew numbered 40 men.

mainmast

Food and other supplies were stored below deck.

foremast

bow

hold

Unwanted passengers

All sailing ships had unwanted passengers:

WEEVILS

FLEAS

MAGGOTS

RATS

23

FERDINAND MAGELLAN

Ferdinand Magellan, born in about 1480 in Portugal, had the same idea as Christopher Columbus. He too believed that he could get to the Spice Islands by sailing west from Europe. Columbus had found that America lay in the way, but Magellan thought he could find a sea passage through.

He needed a sponsor to pay for the voyage. Magellan was Portuguese, but the Portuguese king had treated him badly, so he offered his plan to Charles V, king of Spain.

THE SHIPS
Charles V gave Magellan five ships: the Trinidad, the San Antonio, the Concepcion, the Victoria and the Santiago. They were very small, old and patched up – not fit for a long journey in rough seas, but Magellan took them because they were the best he could get.

THE CREW
Spanish sailors didn't want to serve with Magellan because he was Portuguese. Magellan had to take anyone who would sign on, whether they were skilled seamen or not. Some of the crew were prisoners, released from jail in return for sailing with him.

KEY DATES
- **Sep 1519** Magellan's fleet left Seville in Spain
- **Nov 1519** The ships reached the coast of Brazil
- **Mar 1520** The fleet reached Patagonia
- **Oct 1520** The Magellan Strait was discovered
- **Nov 1520** The ships emerged into the South Pacific
- **Mar 1521** The ships reached Guam
- **Apr 1521** Magellan was killed in the Philippines
- **Sep 1522** The *Victoria* returned to Spain

THE JOURNEY

In September 1519 Magellan and his men said their prayers and set off from southern Spain. At first all went well. The little fleet reached South America and stocked up with fresh food. Then they sailed down the coast of South America, looking for a passage through, but they couldn't find a strait (a strip of water) to let them through from the Atlantic to the Pacific. They had to sail further and further south towards the South Pole. Winter was coming on, the weather was becoming colder and they were running out of food.

The crew mutinied. Magellan hanged the leaders and continued the search. At last, in October 1520, they found a strait. Magellan named it after himself and you can still see it on the map today: the Magellan Strait. It took 38 days to sail through to the Pacific, then they found themselves sailing for weeks on end with no sign of land. The drinking water was stinking and slimy and the crew had to eat rats. One of the captains deserted and sailed his ship, the *San Antonio*, back to Spain.

In March they landed at Guam. Then the ships headed for the Moluccas, the Spice Islands, but Magellan never got there. He was caught up in a native war in the Philippines and died with a spear through his heart.

By now, only three ships remained. One was left behind. The other two reached the Molucca Islands and loaded a rich cargo of spices to take back to Spain. One of these was taken captive. Only one ship, the *Victoria*, reached home. This was the first ship to have sailed right around the world.

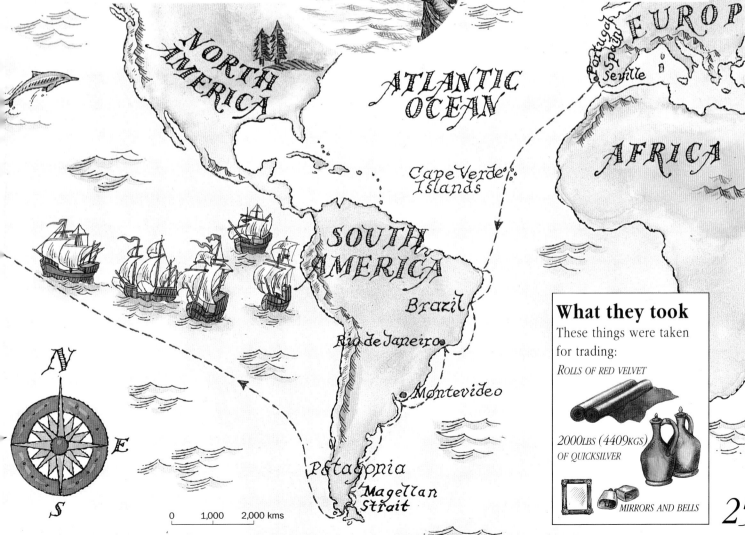

What they took

These things were taken for trading:

ROLLS OF RED VELVET

2000LBS (4409KGS) OF QUICKSILVER

MIRRORS AND BELLS

25

MUTINY ON BOARD

Life was hard on board ship. Sailors spent all their time on deck, working, sleeping and eating there. Towards the end of a long journey, food became very scarce: on Magellan's voyage the crew had to eat rotten biscuits, ox hides and even rats and sawdust. Anyone who fell asleep on watch was whipped or ducked in the sea.

The men who sailed on these long journeys were often very afraid. They believed that they might come to the ends of the Earth or that they might sail on and on until they ran out of food and water. Sometimes, when they had travelled for many days without sight of land, they made plans to kill the captain and turn back. This was called mutiny; it was the worst crime of all on board ship. The penalty was death.

The captains of the *Concepcion* and the *Victoria* mutinied against Magellan. They were hanged, drawn and quartered. Another man who had joined in the mutiny wasn't killed, as he was a representative of the king. Instead he was marooned (left behind) on a desert island.

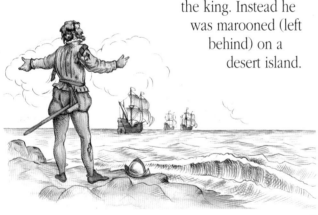

SCURVY

Food was a problem at sea because it could not be kept fresh. At the start of a journey, a ship took on board fresh fruit and vegetables, but these had to be eaten before they went bad. Sometimes the men were at sea for months at a time with no fresh food, so they had no vitamin C in their diet. This often caused a terrible disease called scurvy. First the sailors' gums became sore; then they began to bleed. The sailors' gums turned black and their teeth fell out. They couldn't chew their food because their teeth hurt. The first thing a captain did when his ship anchored was to send ashore for vegetables and fresh fruit to give to seamen suffering from scurvy.

PEOPLE THEY MET

Travelling down the coast of Patagonia, the southernmost part of South America, Magellan's crew met an enormous man who was dancing and singing all alone. He was so tall that their heads hardly reached his waist. He wore big shoes made of skin.

When Magellan's ships reached Guam, the islanders came out in canoes to welcome them. They brought coconut and fruit to trade for iron. Their intention was to be friendly to the foreigners, but Magellan thought they were stealing. He ordered his crossbow men to open fire and several of the islanders were killed.

WHAT HAPPENED TO THE SHIPS

The *Santiago* was lost in a storm off Patagonia; the *San Antonio* was taken back to Spain, taking most of the supplies with her; the *Concepcion* was burned by the crew after Magellan died, as there were not enough men left alive to sail her home; the *Trinidad* was taken captive by the Portuguese, who had taken possession of the Spice Islands; the *Victoria* was the only ship to get safely home to Spain.

Out of five ships, one returned. Out of 250 men, 18 came back.

HERNANDO CORTES AND THE AZTECS

The Aztec empire stretched over an area of North America that now belongs to Mexico. From the capital of Tenochtitlán, which is now Mexico City, ruled the emperor, Montezuma. He lived in a palace with 1,000 wives and he was so holy that he never put his feet on the ground. He was carried everywhere.

In the cities, the Aztecs held big markets which sold corn, beans, jewels, weapons, cloaks made of feathers and little hairless dogs, which the Aztec people ate. There were also peppers, tomatoes and avocado pears for sale. You could buy cocoa beans there to make into chocolate, but this was so precious that it was kept for very special occasions.

THE AZTEC GODS

The Aztecs believed in many different gods: Tláloc, the god of rain, was probably the oldest god. His sister or wife was the goddess of running water. She also protected marriage and new-born babies. There were several gods of farming: Centéotl was the god of maize and Chicomecóatl was the goddess of corn. Quetzalcóatl (shown

above) was the god of the wind and the arts. The war god, Huitzilopochtli, was one of the most important Aztec gods.

AZTECS AND THE SUN GOD

The Aztecs worshipped the Sun. They believed that there had once been five suns and that, one by one, they had all died, until there was just one left. It could only be kept alive by offerings of blood.

Every day, Aztec men, women and children pricked their ear with a cactus spine to make it bleed. They offered the drops of blood to the Sun God.

Aztec priests sacrificed prisoners of war. They cut open their chests and offered their hearts to the Sun God. The Aztecs believed that the sacrificed people did not die, but went up into the sky to live in happiness with the Sun God.

Mexico City (Tenochtitlán)

KEY DATES
- **Feb 1519** Cortés landed in North America
- **Nov 1519** His army entered Tenochtitlán
- **Jul 1520** His army fought their way out of the city
- **May-Aug 1521** Cortés besieged the city

PACIFIC OCEAN

HERNANDO CORTES

Hernando Cortés came from Spain. He was a *conquistador* (an adventurer and conqueror) who went to North America to seek his fortune. When he landed in Veracruz in 1519, he burnt his boats to show his men there was no turning back and marched to the Aztec capital, Tenochtitlán.

The Aztecs had never seen strangers like these men who rode on monsters (horses) and carried sticks which spat thunder (guns). Their faces were pale and their skins hairy, and the Aztecs took them for gods.

Cortés and his army reached the capital on 8th November 1519. Montezuma sent them presents and allowed them to enter the city. He even gave them rooms in his own palace. As time passed, however, the Aztecs realised their mistake.

The Spaniards began to attack the Aztec nobles and kill them for their gold. The Aztecs rose up against the Spaniards. Montezuma tried to calm them, but was stoned by his own people and died soon after.

Cortés' army fought their way out of Tenochtitlán over the bodies of the dead. When Cortés returned with more men, he found the Aztecs weakened by hunger and disease. After a four-month siege, the Spaniards took the city. The Aztec empire was at an end.

FRANCISCO PIZARRO AND THE INCAS

High up in the Andes, in the country which is now called Peru, there was once a great empire. It was ruled by the Inca – an emperor who was worshipped by his people as a god. The people of his empire are also known to us as the Incas.

The Inca empire was very rich. It stretched for thousands of kilometres. In the capital, Cuzco, stood the emperor's palace and the temple of the Sun. It was covered with sheets of gold. Gold, the Incas believed, was the sweat of the Sun.

The emperor controlled everything. He told his people when to plant and when to harvest, when to make roads and when to go to war.

The Incas built bridges and roads, which went over the high mountains. The emperor's messengers travelled the roads by foot as they had no animals to carry them. The Incas had no form of writing, so the runners carried messages in their heads. They also had a knotted rope called a *quipu*. Every knot had a special meaning and these could be 'read'.

Orinoco

Colombia

SOUTH AMERICA

Amazon

Brazil

Cuzco

Lake Titicaca

KEY DATES
- **1530** Pizarro landed in Peru
- **Nov 1532** The Spaniards took Atahualpa prisoner
- **Aug 1533** The Spaniards killed Atahualpa

FRANCISCO PIZARRO

Pizarro was a Spanish conquistador. He set out in 1530 for Peru with 180 men and 37 horses to make his fortune. He and his army landed on the west coast of Peru and then began the long climb into the Andes mountains. They were met by a messenger and guide from Atahualpa, the emperor of the Incas, and led to the hot springs where Atahualpa and his court were relaxing.

Although the Spaniards were greatly outnumbered by the soldiers and courtiers of the emperor, they turned on the astonished Incas with their swords and guns, killing thousands of them. Atahualpa himself was captured by Pizarro.

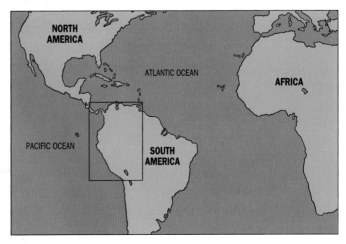

Atahualpa saw that the Spaniards loved gold. He offered to give Pizarro a whole room filled with gold in exchange for his freedom. Pizarro agreed, so Atahualpa sent out word to his people. The Incas stripped their temples to pay the ransom. However, when the room was full, Pizarro broke his promise and had the emperor killed. The Inca empire fell apart and the Spanish became the new rulers of Peru.

NORTH AMERICA

ATLANTIC OCEAN

AFRICA

PACIFIC OCEAN

SOUTH AMERICA

THE EXPLORERS OF NORTH AMERICA

Spain and Portugal had sent out more successful explorers than any other country. Following Vasco da Gama's success in reaching India from Portugal, the Portuguese were able to use the route to the Spice Islands that took them around the southern tip of Africa. The Spanish had shown that there was no easy way to the Far East through South America. Other European countries, such as Britain, France and Holland, were keen to send out explorers to new areas. One of these areas was North America, where the land was rich and easy to farm and the seas were full of fish. In the north there were forests to provide wood and beavers and deer to hunt for fur; further south were herds of wild buffalo. The main reason, however, for sending explorers to North America was to try and find another route to the Spice Islands.

HENRY HUDSON

Hudson was English, but he worked for a Dutch trading company called the Dutch East India Company. They thought there might be a passage to the Far East through North America and they sent Hudson to look.

Hudson made two great journeys. In 1609 he sailed up the east coast of North America, looking for a way through into the Pacific. He found a great river, which is now named after him: the Hudson River. He did not find a passage.

In 1610 he set out again. This time he was working for the English. He sailed much further north and found a strait (a way through) and a great bay, both of which now bear his name. As winter came on, the Hudson Bay froze over and his ship, the *Discovery*, was trapped. The crew mutinied and Hudson, his son and seven sailors were cast adrift. They were never heard of again.

KEY DATES
- **1603-15** Champlain explored Canada
- **1609** Hudson found the Hudson River
- **1610** Hudson discovered the Hudson Bay and the Hudson Strait
- **1797-1812** Thompson explored the northwest of North America
- **1806** Lewis and Clark reached the Pacific coast of North America

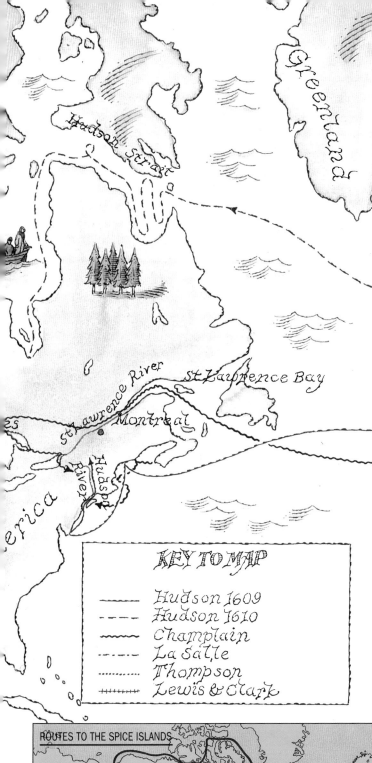

OVERLAND EXPLORERS

The French sent Samuel de Champlain (shown below) to explore Canada. Between 1603 and 1615, he explored the St Lawrence River and the Great Lakes. He was guided by Indians and travelled much of the way by canoe. Champlain found the way for the French fur traders, who later settled in Canada.

Another Frenchman, Robert Cavelier, Sieur de la Salle, sailed from the Great Lakes down the Mississippi River and, in 1681, became the first European to reach its mouth. He claimed all the land of the Mississippi basin for France and named the new land Louisiana, in honour of the French king, Louis XIV.

Between 1797 and 1812, David Thompson explored the northwest and crossed the Rocky Mountains. He worked for an English trading company and was one of the first explorers to make really accurate maps.

In 1804 Meriwether Lewis and William Clark sailed up the Missouri River and rode over the Rocky Mountains, reaching the Pacific coast two years later. They were Americans, sent by their President, Thomas Jefferson.

KEY TO MAP

—————— Hudson 1609
– – – – – Hudson 1610
∿∿∿∿∿ Champlain
–·–·–·– La Salle
·············· Thompson
+++++++ Lewis & Clark

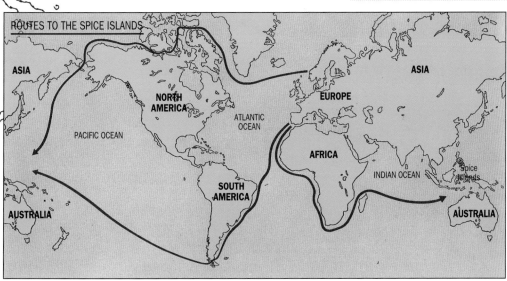

ROUTES TO THE SPICE ISLANDS

What they brought back

FURS AND BUFFALO SKINS

TOBACCO

POTATOES

NATIVES FEATHER AND BEAD WORK

33

THE PEOPLE OF NORTH AMERICA

To begin with, most native Americans were friendly to the Europeans. They thought there was plenty of land and food for everybody. The very first settlers, the Pilgrim Fathers who sailed to America from England in 1620, were helped by Samoset and Squanto, two people of the Masasoit tribe. They showed the white men how to plant corn and set fish traps.

Pocahontas (shown right) was a native American princess. Her father had captured an Englishman called John Smith and threatened to kill him. Pocahontas begged for his life and saved him. Sacajawea was a woman of the Shoshoni tribe. She guided Lewis and Clark along the Missouri to the Columbia River.

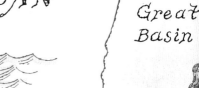

NATIVE AMERICAN CUSTOMS

Native American children were expected to be brave. When they were only three or four, they were tattooed with bone needles and plunged into icy rivers to make them tough.

When local tribes went to war, they painted themselves and their horses in order to look fierce. Before they set out, they danced a war dance. The medicine man worked magic to try to make sure his side won. Before the arrival of the Europeans, the people did not have horses or guns. In battle they used bows, arrows and *tomahawks* (axes made of stone). The horses and guns introduced by the Europeans made a big difference to the native inhabitants' way of life. The hunting tribes quickly learnt to use them to catch buffalo. The wheeled transport introduced by the Europeans replaced the stretchers used by the native people to drag heavy objects along.

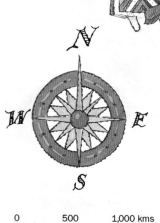

0   500   1,000 kms

THE NATIVE PEOPLE

THE ARCTIC
In the Arctic lived the Inuit (Eskimos). They were hunters and fishers: they speared seals through holes made in the ice and made boats of seal skin called *kayaks*, which they used for fishing in the summer. In the winter they hunted polar bears in sledges pulled by husky dogs.

THE NORTHWEST COAST
The people of the northwest coast were expert fishermen. They travelled in dugout canoes, which were often beautifully carved.

THE GREAT BASIN
The tribes of the Great Basin were very poor. They lived on the seeds they gathered from the dusty land.

THE GREAT PLAINS
The people of the Plains followed the buffalo herds. When it was time for a hunt, the whole tribe set off together. Medicine men sang and danced to bring out the buffalo. The native people ate dried buffalo meat and their tents, or *teepees*, were made of buffalo skin.

THE SOUTHWEST
The tribes of the southwest were farmers. They made beautiful pottery and baskets. Some tribes wove wonderful cloth. Their medicine men made pictures out of sand to help them work magic.

THE NORTHEAST
The northeast of America was covered with thick forest. The people here lived by hunting

and fishing, but they also farmed in small clearings in the forest. Their houses and canoes were made of birch bark. They made and traded *wampum* – belts made of shells which they used as money.

35

THE EXPLORERS OF SOUTH AMERICA

The first explorers of South America were the Spanish conquistadors, whose search was for gold. Until the 18th century, South America, claimed by Spain, was practically unknown to explorers from other countries. Then, at last, the search for gold was replaced by a search for scientific knowledge. The new explorers wanted to find out about the rich animal and plant life. Their journeys took them deep into the rainforest, where they faced danger at every step: thick jungle hid poisonous snakes, jaguars and hostile tribes, but the greatest danger to the Europeans was of catching illness and fever.

ALEXANDER VON HUMBOLDT

This German explorer was rich enough to pay for his own expedition in 1799. He was keen to learn all he could about South America and travelled all over the continent, often at great risk. He explored the Orinoco River, climbed the high Andes Mountains, peered into the mouth of a live volcano and got a shock from an electric eel. One of his discoveries was the Humboldt Current – a cold sea current off the coast of Peru.

Humboldt was interested in the people of South America. He saw that they were often treated badly by the Europeans. When he returned home, he worked hard to tell people about this and to help bring about change.

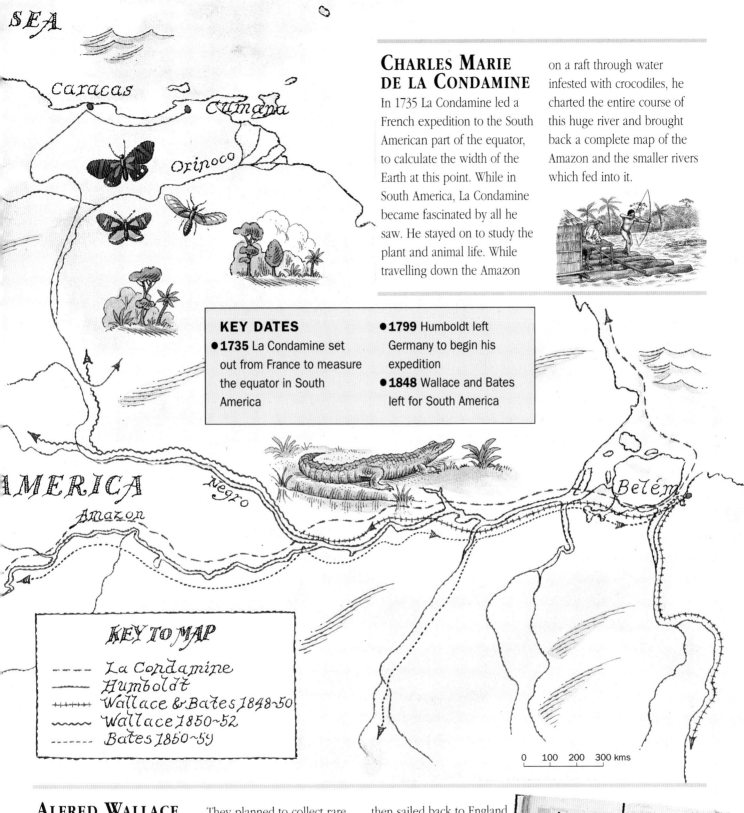

CHARLES MARIE DE LA CONDAMINE

In 1735 La Condamine led a French expedition to the South American part of the equator, to calculate the width of the Earth at this point. While in South America, La Condamine became fascinated by all he saw. He stayed on to study the plant and animal life. While travelling down the Amazon on a raft through water infested with crocodiles, he charted the entire course of this huge river and brought back a complete map of the Amazon and the smaller rivers which fed into it.

KEY DATES
- **1735** La Condamine set out from France to measure the equator in South America
- **1799** Humboldt left Germany to begin his expedition
- **1848** Wallace and Bates left for South America

KEY TO MAP
- - - - - - La Condamine
———— Humboldt
+++++++ Wallace & Bates 1848~50
〜〜〜 Wallace 1850~52
- - - - - Bates 1850~59

0   100   200   300 kms

ALFRED WALLACE AND HENRY BATES

These two friends from England were both keen naturalists (people who study animals and plants). In 1848 they set off for South America on a collecting expedition. They planned to collect rare specimens to sell in England and, in this way, they hoped to be able to pay for the trip.

For three years they travelled together, studying plants and creatures they had never seen before. Wallace then sailed back to England, but he lost most of his collection when his ship caught fire. Bates stayed on in South America until 1859, writing about and sketching hundreds of new specimens.

37

EXPLORING SOUTH AMERICA

The explorers who travelled down the Amazon were the first Europeans to enter the rainforests. For the most part they travelled by raft or canoe. It was an environment unlike anything they had ever seen before.

The waters of the Amazon were full of life. There were alligators five metres long, large swimming rodents called capybara, water snakes and turtles. In places there were piranha fish, which could strip a man's arm to the bone in ten minutes, and shoals of sting rays. Electric eels lurked in the shallows. When Humboldt accidentally stepped on one, it took him a whole day to recover.

Flocks of flamingoes and spoonbills flew overhead. In the trees were howler monkeys and parrots; sloths hung upside-down from the branches. There was the danger of jaguars and pumas. At night, there were vampire bats which sucked the blood of many types of creature. One of these even bit Humboldt's pet dog.

Venezuela

Colombia

Magdalena

Orinoco

Rio Negro

Ecuador

Amaz

Peru

Brazil

Andes Mountains

SOUTH AMERICA

PACIFIC OCEAN

Paraguay

Paraná

Chile

Argentina

Patagonia

Falkland Islands

Strait of Magella

Tierra del Fuego

What they brought back

The explorers of South America brought back:

RUBBER

GOLD

PLATINUM

MAHOGANY

0   500   1,000 kms

THE PEOPLE OF SOUTH AMERICA

Deep in the jungle of South America lived many different tribes of native Americans. They lived mainly by farming, growing crops such as cassava, beans, corn, squash and sweet potato. Cassava was their most important crop, although its roots contain poison. The native people removed the poison by grating and squeezing the roots. They ground the remains into meal for making bread.

The different tribes often fought with one another. One tribe, the Jívaro, shrunk the heads of captives as trophies; other tribes were cannibals.

The people of several South American tribes covered their bodies with painted designs and wore ornate jewellery. Others made holes in their cheeks with sharp pieces of bone or tattooed themselves all over. Children of the Arua tribe had their ear-lobes stretched by weights. This caused the lobes to hang down, sometimes as far as their shoulders.

The native people knew the rainforest very well. They knew all about the plants: which ones were poisonous and which could be used as food and medicine. They were skilful hunters, killing fish, animals and birds of the rainforest for food. Their weapons included spears, bows and arrows, blowguns, nets, hooks and drugs for stunning fish.

THE RUBBER TREE

The people of the rainforest showed Humboldt a tree which, when cut, oozed a sticky, milk-white sap. This is latex, the sap from which rubber is made.

39

CAPTAIN COOK

Long after the other continents were explored, the Australian continent remained a mystery. For many years people believed there was a huge southern land, which they called 'Terra Australis'. They thought it was a magical place with unicorns and dragons where the rivers ran with jewels.

It took a long time to learn the truth because Australia is so far away from Europe. The Pacific Ocean is vast and it took months for a sailing ship to cross it. Taking enough food and water to last the voyage was also a problem. The exploration of the Pacific could only start when newer, faster sailing ships were developed.

ABEL TASMAN

In 1642 Abel Jansz Tasman, a Dutch captain, was sent to explore the South Pacific. He landed on a small island south of Australia, meeting with fierce resistance from the native people. He named this island Van Diemen's Land after the Governor General of the Dutch East Indies and claimed it for Holland. Nowadays, we call it Tasmania after the Dutch sea captain.

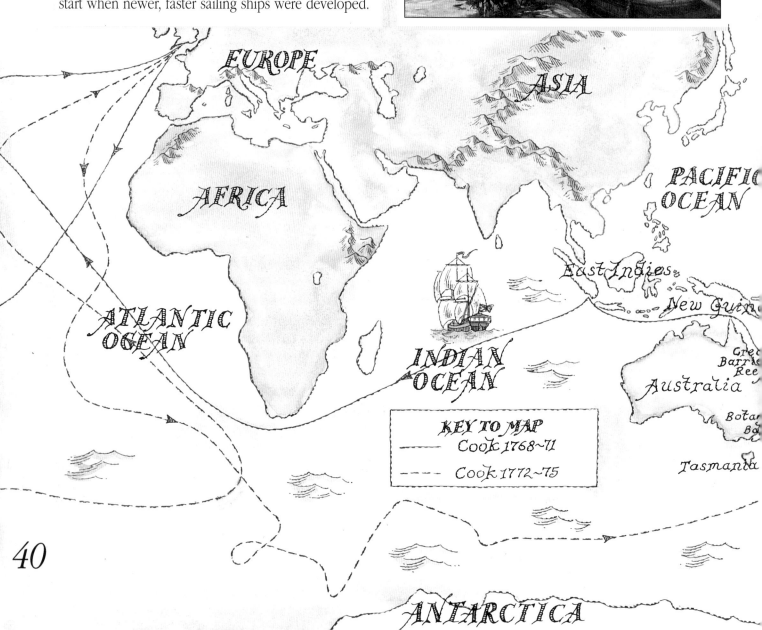

EUROPE

ASIA

AFRICA

PACIFIC OCEAN

ATLANTIC OCEAN

East Indies

New Guin

INDIAN OCEAN

Gre Barr Ree

Australia

Bota Ba

Tasmania

KEY TO MAP
——— Cook 1768~71
- - - - Cook 1772~75

ANTARCTICA

COOK'S FIRST AND SECOND JOURNEYS

James Cook was born the son of a Yorkshire farm worker in 1728. He joined the navy as an ordinary seaman, but rose quickly through the ranks, becoming captain of his first ship in 1767.

In 1768 he set out as leader of a scientific expedition to Tahiti in the Pacific Ocean, from where scientists planned to watch the planet Venus passing in front of the Sun – a very rare event. After this, Cook had orders to explore the unknown continent of Australia, which he knew lay somewhere in the South Pacific.

From Tahiti, he sailed in his ship, the *Endeavour*, all the way to New Zealand, carefully charting the coastline. Then he went on to Australia, landing first at Botany Bay and sailing north towards the Great Barrier Reef, where his boat was shipwrecked. After making

repairs, Cook sailed back to England, arriving in 1771.

For his second voyage in 1772, Cook took two ships, the *Resolution* and the *Adventure*. On this journey he sailed further into the Pacific than any European had before him. He sailed round the Antarctic Circle, meeting many dangers, such

as icebergs, pack-ice, ferocious winds and freezing fog. Cook also charted Tonga and Easter Island and discovered New Caledonia. On his journey home he discovered the South Sandwich Islands and South Georgia in the Atlantic.

JOSEPH BANKS

One of the scientists on Cook's first voyage was Joseph Banks, the chief natural historian. He came from a wealthy family and he brought with him four manservants to look after his clothes and a pair of greyhounds.

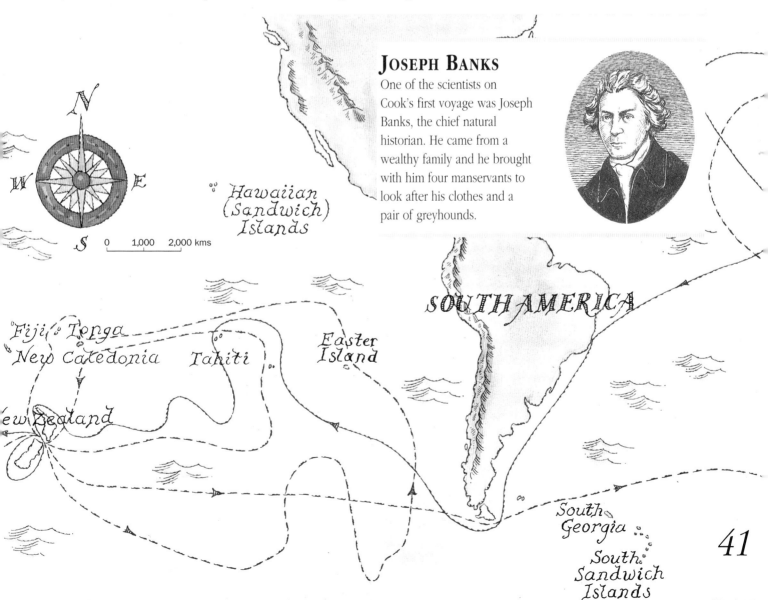

COOK'S FINAL VOYAGE

On his third voyage Cook explored the Pacific Ocean to see how far north he could go. He took two ships, the *Resolution* and the *Discovery*, and in 1776 sailed for the Pacific, where he discovered a number of the islands later  called the Cook Islands and the islands of Hawaii, which he named the Sandwich Islands. In March 1778 he reached the coast of Oregon in North America, and from here he followed the coastline north and west as far as the Bering Strait in the Arctic, where pack-ice forced him to turn back.

The two ships returned to spend the winter in Hawaii. The natives here believed Cook was a god. All went well until one of Cook's men died. The islanders knew then that the sailors were only men like themselves. A little later, trouble broke out over the theft of one of Cook's boats and Cook was killed, clubbed to death by the men who had previously worshipped him.

COOK'S ACHIEVEMENTS

Cook cleared up the mystery of the area known as 'Terra Australis'. He was the first person to sail round Australia and establish its coastline. He charted much of the Pacific Ocean and discovered several island groups.

On his second voyage, Cook took with him a ship's clock called a chronometer. For the first time on a round-the-world voyage, the clock kept going for the length of the journey, allowing Cook to measure accurately the distance of the Earth from east to west (its longitude).

Cook was one of the first sea captains to find an answer to scurvy. Every man in his crew was issued with onions and given the order to eat them. He also gave the sailors pickled cabbage to eat and, when they refused, ordered the officers to eat it to set an example. As a result, not one of his men died from scurvy during his long voyages.

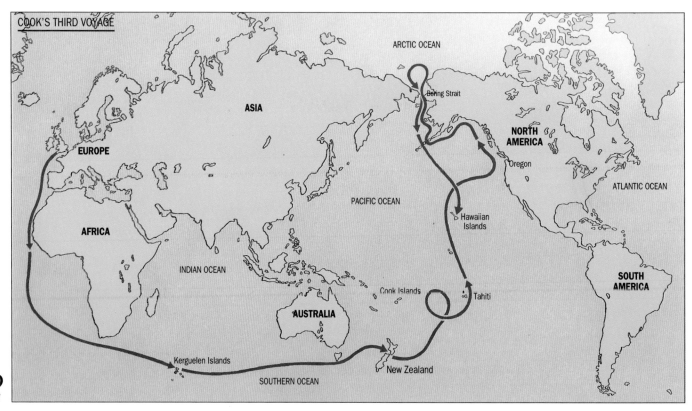

COOK'S THIRD VOYAGE

ARCTIC OCEAN

ASIA

EUROPE

Bering Strait

NORTH AMERICA

Oregon

ATLANTIC OCEAN

PACIFIC OCEAN

Hawaiian Islands

AFRICA

INDIAN OCEAN

Cook Islands

Tahiti

SOUTH AMERICA

AUSTRALIA

Kerguelen Islands

New Zealand

SOUTHERN OCEAN

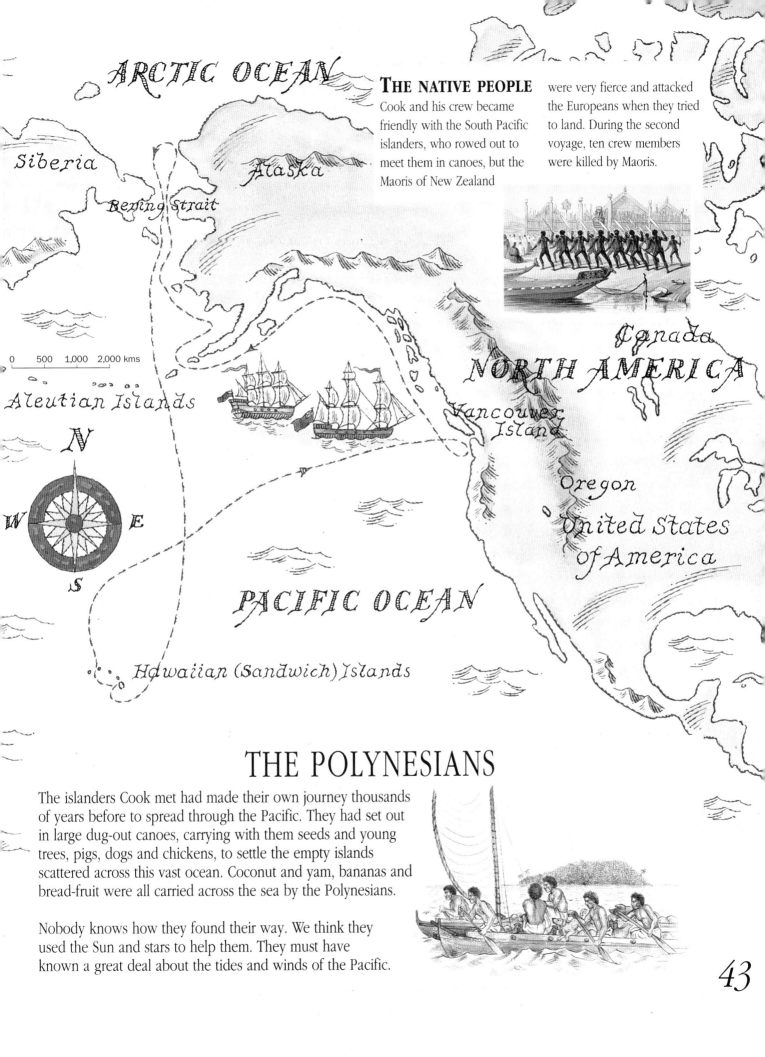

ARCTIC OCEAN

Siberia

Alaska

Bering Strait

Aleutian Islands

0 500 1,000 2,000 kms

N
W   E
S

PACIFIC OCEAN

Hawaiian (Sandwich) Islands

Canada

NORTH AMERICA

Vancouver Island

Oregon

United States of America

THE NATIVE PEOPLE

Cook and his crew became friendly with the South Pacific islanders, who rowed out to meet them in canoes, but the Maoris of New Zealand were very fierce and attacked the Europeans when they tried to land. During the second voyage, ten crew members were killed by Maoris.

THE POLYNESIANS

The islanders Cook met had made their own journey thousands of years before to spread through the Pacific. They had set out in large dug-out canoes, carrying with them seeds and young trees, pigs, dogs and chickens, to settle the empty islands scattered across this vast ocean. Coconut and yam, bananas and bread-fruit were all carried across the sea by the Polynesians.

Nobody knows how they found their way. We think they used the Sun and stars to help them. They must have known a great deal about the tides and winds of the Pacific.

43

THE EXPLORERS OF AUSTRALIA

Captain Cook was English, so the British claimed Australia as their possession. By the late 1790s, Britain was using Australia as a place to send prisoners. This was called transportation.

In the early days, the prisoners and their guards stayed in Botany Bay. Behind the bay lay the mountains. They made it difficult for people to travel far inland. But as the colony became more and more populated, new land began to be needed.

Gregory Blaxland, William Wentworth and William Lawson were the first people to cross the mountains in 1813. They were looking for new country for their animals. They found that good land lay beyond. Soon other settlers followed their lead and spread inland from Botany Bay.

The land was watered by rivers. The settlers believed there must be a great sea or lake somewhere in the centre of Australia. In 1828 Charles Sturt took a rowing boat up the Macquarie River to look for it. He rowed 3,200 kilometres and faced swamps and drought, hostile tribes and deadly snakes. He found no great sea, but he did discover the Darling River.

In 1844 Sturt set out from Adelaide to trace the Murray River. The men crossed a desert so hot and dry that they had to dig shelters against the sun. The journey lasted 17 months and began to open up the middle of Australia to the European settlers.

INDIAN OCEAN

Darwin

Great Sandy Desert

KEY TO MAP

- - - - - Blaxland, Wentworth & Lawson
· · · · · · · Sturt 1828~29
———— Sturt 1844
—· —· — Burke
~~~~~ Stuart

Great Victoria Desert

0   200   400 kms

Perth

PEOPLE OF THE BUSH

The bush is the name given to the sparse, uncultivated countryside of Australia and, for the Europeans, it was very dangerous. But the Aborigines knew it well and could find food and water even in the hottest and driest parts. They knew where to look for wild figs and bush tomatoes, honey ants and witchetty grubs. The men fished and hunted kangaroo with spear throwers called *woomeras*. The women and children gathered berries.

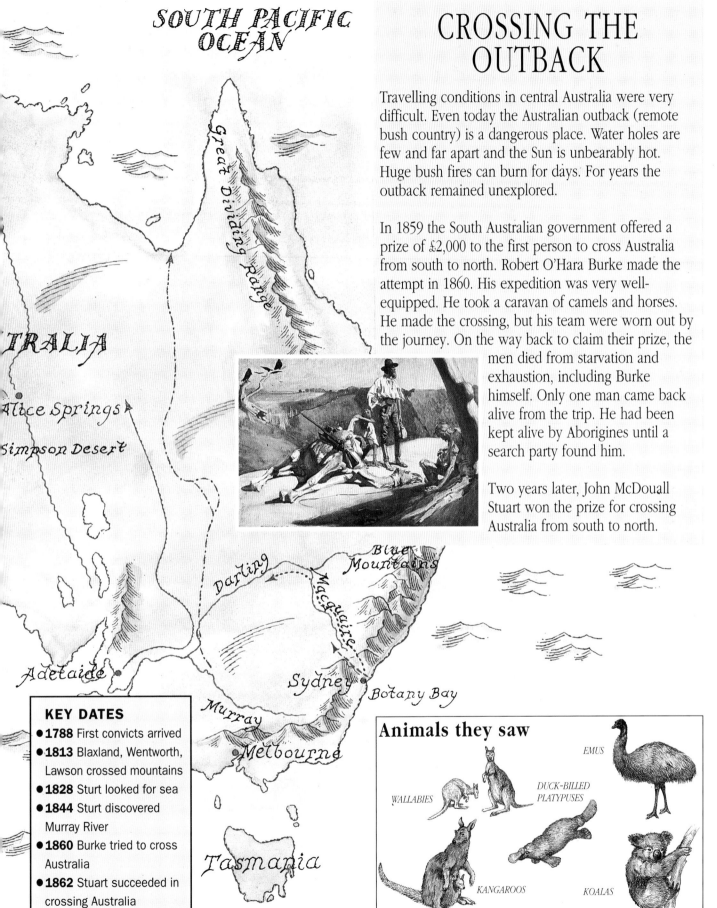

SOUTH PACIFIC OCEAN

Great Dividing Range

RALIA

Alice Springs

Simpson Desert

Darling

Blue Mountains

Macquarie

Adelaide

Sydney

Botany Bay

Murray

Melbourne

Tasmania

CROSSING THE OUTBACK

Travelling conditions in central Australia were very difficult. Even today the Australian outback (remote bush country) is a dangerous place. Water holes are few and far apart and the Sun is unbearably hot. Huge bush fires can burn for days. For years the outback remained unexplored.

In 1859 the South Australian government offered a prize of £2,000 to the first person to cross Australia from south to north. Robert O'Hara Burke made the attempt in 1860. His expedition was very well-equipped. He took a caravan of camels and horses. He made the crossing, but his team were worn out by the journey. On the way back to claim their prize, the men died from starvation and exhaustion, including Burke himself. Only one man came back alive from the trip. He had been kept alive by Aborigines until a search party found him.

Two years later, John McDouall Stuart won the prize for crossing Australia from south to north.

KEY DATES

- **1788** First convicts arrived
- **1813** Blaxland, Wentworth, Lawson crossed mountains
- **1828** Sturt looked for sea
- **1844** Sturt discovered Murray River
- **1860** Burke tried to cross Australia
- **1862** Stuart succeeded in crossing Australia

Animals they saw

WALLABIES

DUCK-BILLED PLATYPUSES

EMUS

KANGAROOS

KOALAS

45

THE EXPLORERS OF AFRICA

Long before the Europeans entered Africa, the Arabs were trading there. The continent was criss-crossed with trade routes used by the Arab merchants. They brought salt and gold with them, which they traded for ivory and slaves. They carried the goods in camel caravans. Sometimes as many as 1,000 camels made the journey. These caravans crossed deserts and high mountains, travelling vast distances to reach the great markets of Africa.

The first Europeans to settle in Africa were the Dutch. They settled in the Cape of Good Hope in 1652. Gradually they spread further north and, in 1760, an elephant hunter called Jacob Coetsee crossed the Orange River. Once they had crossed this natural barrier, the Europeans began to spread out across South Africa.

To begin with, Europeans went to Africa to trade, especially in slaves. Then they went as hunters, many of them killing elephants for their ivory. Later still came the missionaries, who wanted to teach the Africans to pray to the Christian god. Some also tried to end the slave trade.

RENE-AUGUSTE CAILLIE

On the southern edge of the Sahara Desert in North Africa is the city of Timbuktu. This was one of the most important trading centres of Africa. To the Europeans it was known as 'the forbidden city' because the Muslim Arabs did not allow Christians to enter. The French Geographical Society offered a prize to the first person to get into Timbuktu and a young Frenchman, René-Auguste Caillié, decided to try. He learnt to speak Arabic and he studied the Muslim Holy Book, the *Qu'ran*.

In March 1827 he disguised himself as a Muslim and then travelled to the west coast of Africa.

There he joined a salt caravan on its way to Timbuktu. After two months on the road he collapsed with malaria and scurvy. The old woman who looked after him guessed he was not a Muslim, but she kept his secret. In March 1828, an entire year after setting out, the caravan reached Djenné, where they boarded a boat for Timbuktu.

It was another 800 kilometres before Caillié got his first glimpse of Timbuktu. He entered the city, but by now he was in danger as his disguise was beginning to arouse suspicion. He managed to escape over the Atlas Mountains and get back to France to claim his prize.

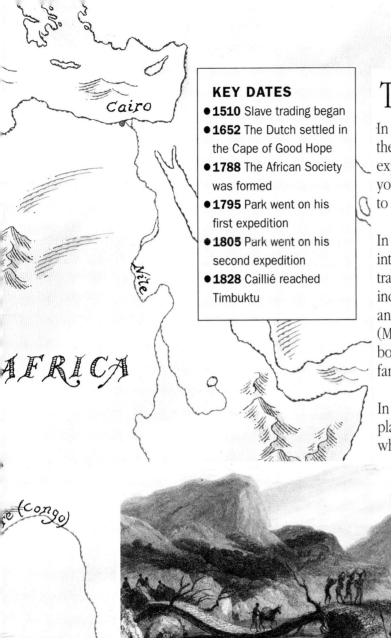

KEY DATES on map:
- Cairo
- Nile
- AFRICA
- (Congo)
- Zambezi
- N E S (compass)
- Orange
- INDIAN OCEAN
- Cape of Good Hope

KEY DATES

- **1510** Slave trading began
- **1652** The Dutch settled in the Cape of Good Hope
- **1788** The African Society was formed
- **1795** Park went on his first expedition
- **1805** Park went on his second expedition
- **1828** Caillié reached Timbuktu

KEY TO MAP
- ~~~~ Park 1795~96
- ---- Park 1805~6
- ······ Caillié

0   500   1,000 kms

THE AFRICAN SOCIETY

In 1788 a group of rich Britons formed the African Society. Its aim was to explore Africa. The Society hired a young Scottish doctor, Mungo Park, to make the first expedition.

In 1795 Park took with him two interpreters and some presents for trading. He endured many hardships, including suffering from extreme hunger and thirst and being taken prisoner by Muslims of North Africa (Moors). When he returned to Scotland he wrote a book about his travels. Before long he became very famous.

In May 1805 Park began his second expedition. He planned to travel down the River Niger to the sea, which would make him the first European to do so. He started down the Falémé River with 44 men, but by August, when he reached the Niger, only ten men were still alive; disease had killed the rest. By November, there were only five left. That was the last that was heard of Mungo Park. He never reached the mouth of the Niger.

Five years later, a Mandingo guide went to find out what had happened. He learnt that Park and his men had crossed into Hausa Country. The boat they were in was holed by rapids. At the same time they were attacked by tribesmen. The Europeans did not survive the attack and the fierce river currents.

Animals they saw

The Europeans saw animals they had never seen before, such as:

ELEPHANTS

GIRAFFES

ZEBRAS

47

BURTON AND SPEKE

At the far north of Africa, the mighty river Nile spreads out into the Mediterranean Sea. The oldest maps plot its route through Egypt, but until the middle of the 19th century its source (the place where the river begins) was a mystery. Ivory traders told of a great lake in the centre of Africa,

filled by the melting snow from a high range of mountains, but when European explorers tried to trace the river back to the mountains, waterfalls and rapids blocked their way.

In 1856 Britain's Royal Geographical Society raised £1,000 to pay for an expedition to search for the source of the Nile. As leaders, they chose Richard Burton and John Speke, both English army officers. The Society instructed them to look for the great lake by travelling inland from the island of Zanzibar on Africa's east coast. Then they were to go north to the mountains in search of the source of the Nile.

TRAVELLING BY LAND

Burton and Speke took so much luggage with them on their journeys that they needed 130 porters and 30 donkeys to carry it all. Nevertheless, they lost much of it as they crossed dangerous rivers and swamps. While they were travelling, both men became very ill, and the porters had to carry them, as well as the luggage.

Hoggar Mountains

Sahara Desert

AFRIC

0   200   400 kms

KEY TO MAP
Burton & Speke
------ Speke

AFRICAN DISEASES

Today's visitors to Africa safeguard their health with modern drugs, but in the 19th century Europeans found the climate so unhealthy that they nicknamed the continent 'the white man's grave'. The medicine brought by Burton and Speke was no protection against malaria and fever. Burton's legs became paralysed

and useless, and a small beetle crawled into Speke's ear, causing a horrible infection. For a time he was quite blind, and could not see Lake Tanganyika when the expedition reached it.

N
W   E
S

Za

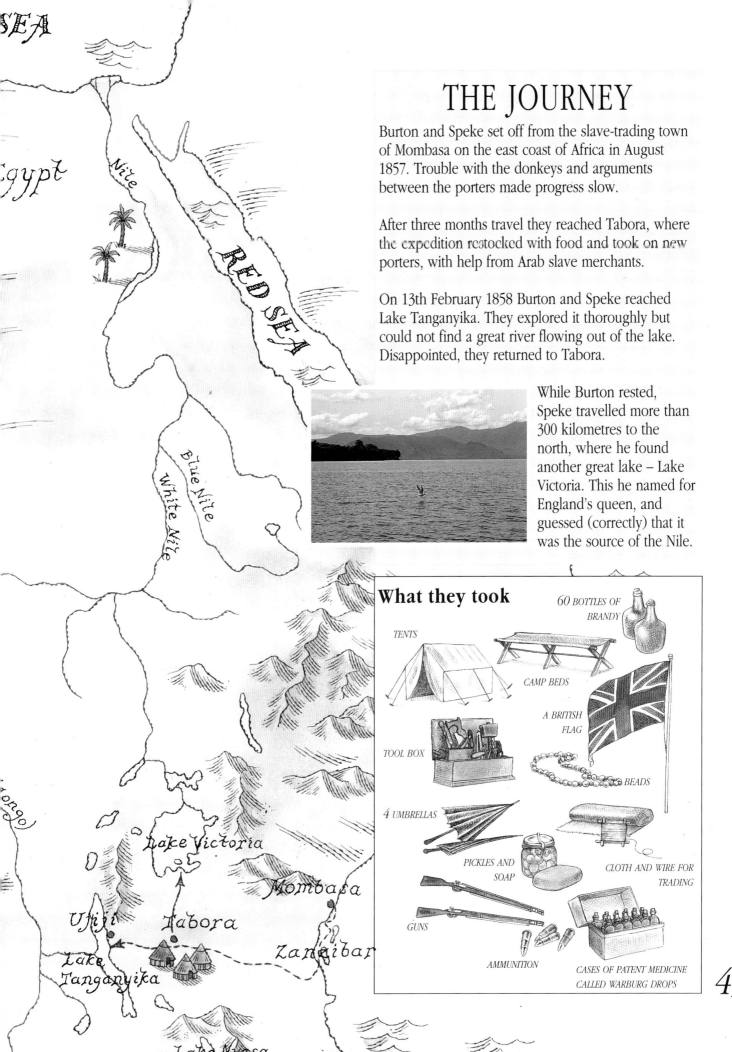

THE JOURNEY

Burton and Speke set off from the slave-trading town of Mombasa on the east coast of Africa in August 1857. Trouble with the donkeys and arguments between the porters made progress slow.

After three months travel they reached Tabora, where the expedition restocked with food and took on new porters, with help from Arab slave merchants.

On 13th February 1858 Burton and Speke reached Lake Tanganyika. They explored it thoroughly but could not find a great river flowing out of the lake. Disappointed, they returned to Tabora.

While Burton rested, Speke travelled more than 300 kilometres to the north, where he found another great lake – Lake Victoria. This he named for England's queen, and guessed (correctly) that it was the source of the Nile.

What they took

60 BOTTLES OF BRANDY

TENTS

CAMP BEDS

A BRITISH FLAG

TOOL BOX

BEADS

4 UMBRELLAS

PICKLES AND SOAP

CLOTH AND WIRE FOR TRADING

GUNS

AMMUNITION

CASES OF PATENT MEDICINE CALLED WARBURG DROPS

Map labels: SEA, Egypt, Nile, RED SEA, Blue Nile, White Nile, (ongo), Lake Victoria, Mombasa, Ujiji, Tabora, Zanzibar, Lake Tanganyika, Lake Nyasa

49

LIVINGSTONE AND STANLEY

David Livingstone, the most famous explorer of Africa, was missing. In 1866 he had left Britain to look for the source of the River Nile. Five years later, nothing had been heard of him. An American newspaper called the *New York Herald* sent out its best reporter, Henry Stanley, with the command, 'Find Livingstone!'

Stanley took with him a huge caravan of pack animals and porters. He marched for eight months through deserts and swamps until he came to the town of Ujiji near Lake Tanganyika. There he found David Livingstone, tired, ill and dressed in rags. Taking off his hat, Stanley said the now famous words 'Dr Livingstone, I presume?' He had travelled halfway across Africa to find the man he was looking for.

DAVID LIVINGSTONE

Born in Scotland in 1813 to a poor family, David Livingstone was interested in natural history as a boy. Later he studied medicine, then became a minister with the London Missionary Society.

Livingstone first went to Africa in 1840 to teach the people who lived there about the Christian god. He wanted to open up more routes to the interior of Africa so that other missionaries could reach the local people. He crossed southern Africa from west to east (the first European to do so) and sailed down the Zambezi River. He crossed the Kalahari Desert, where the ground was so dry his party had to dig down three metres before they found water.

He was the first European to see the Victoria Falls, which the Africans called the 'Smoke that Thunders', and to discover Lake Nyasa. He spent half of his life exploring and in 1873, exhausted and ill, he died on the shores of Lake Tanganyika.

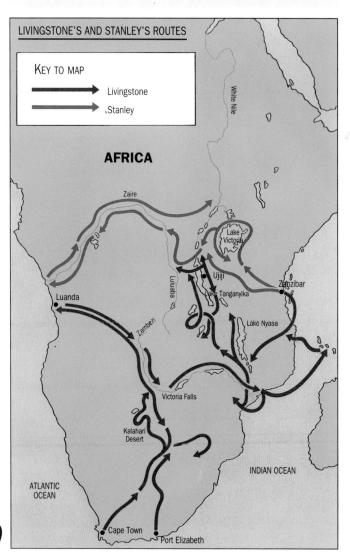

LIVINGSTONE'S AND STANLEY'S ROUTES

KEY TO MAP

→ Livingstone

→ Stanley

AFRICA

White Nile

Zaire

Lake Victoria

Luluaba

Ujiji

Lake Tanganyika

Zanzibar

Luanda

Zambezi

Lake Nyasa

Victoria Falls

Kalahari Desert

ATLANTIC OCEAN

INDIAN OCEAN

Cape Town

Port Elizabeth

HENRY MORTON STANLEY

Born in 1841, Stanley spent his childhood in a workhouse in Wales. He ran away to sea and made his home in America. Later he got a job writing for a newspaper called the *New York Herald*. After his meeting with Livingstone, he went on exploring and sailed down the Zaïre River deep into unknown Africa. He emerged on the west coast after 999 days in the interior. His boat, the *Lady Alice*, was made in sections so that it could be taken apart and carried across or around dangerous parts of the river.

Livingstone took only a few things on his journey across Africa. These were:

4 GUNS TO SHOOT GAME TO FEED HIS PARTY

BEADS FOR TRADING

A SMALL TENT

SPARE CLOTHES

His most precious possessions were:

HIS DIARY

A MEDICINE CHEST

SCIENTIFIC INSTRUMENTS

Stanley took far more. The porters carrying his possessions were arranged by size and age:

SHORT ONES CARRIED SACKS OF BEADS.

TALL ONES CARRIED BALES OF CLOTH.

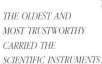

THE OLDEST AND MOST TRUSTWORTHY CARRIED THE SCIENTIFIC INSTRUMENTS.

LIVINGSTONE AND THE AFRICANS

Livingstone spent much of his life fighting against slavery. He was much loved by the Africans because he was so concerned about them and did all he could to help them. He always carried a medicine chest with him and used his skills as a doctor to heal sick people when he met them on his travels.

He had two African servants, Susi and Chuma, who went with him everywhere. These two men stayed with him until he died. Then they carried his body, which they had preserved with salt, for hundreds of kilometres, through swamp and forest, back to Zanzibar on the coast, so that it could be buried in his own country. His heart, though, they buried in Africa.

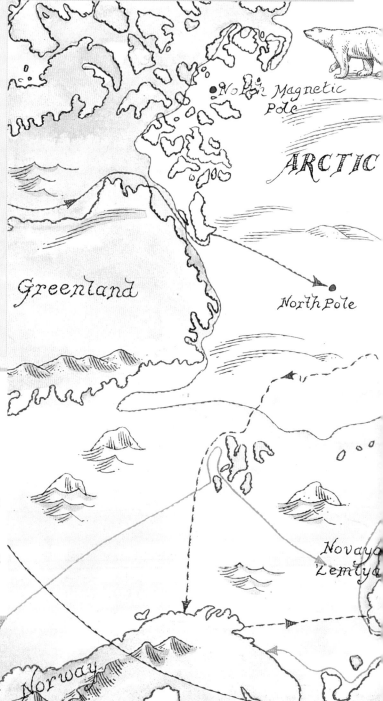

THE EXPLORERS OF THE NORTH POLE

At the top of the world lies the coldest ocean on Earth. It is the Arctic Ocean, where the water freezes into solid ice which can trap a ship forever.

For thousands of years people have known about the Arctic Ocean and its dangers. The Ancient Greeks had explored this area and they believed it marked the end of the Earth.

Europeans began to explore it a few years after Columbus, da Gama and Magellan made their great journeys of discovery. The captains of these European expeditions were looking for a northern passage to the Spice Islands. Spain and Portugal had claimed the two best routes by going south and other nations hoped to find a different way by going far north.

ROBERT PEARY

In 1909 two men took part in a race to reach the North Pole: Robert Peary and Dr Frederick Cook were both Americans. Peary planned his expedition very carefully. He took 133 dogs and twelve sledges and used Inuit (Eskimo) guides. On 6th April 1909, he reached the North Pole with his black servant and friend, Matthew Henson, and four Inuit. Dr Cook later claimed he had reached the Pole before Peary, but people now believe that he was mistaken.

FRIDTJOF NANSEN

Nansen was a Norwegian, born in 1861. He knew that the waters of the Arctic, though frozen, moved very slowly, and believed that if he built a boat strong enough to withstand the ice, he could drift in it towards the North Pole. The attempt in his ship, the *Fram,* took three years and, though it didn't reach the Pole, it taught other explorers much about living in the Arctic.

KEY TO MAP

———	Barents
– – – –	Bering
— – — –	Nansen
———	Peary

aska

Bering Strait

Siberia

OCEAN

Arctic Circle

ASIA

KEY DATES

- **1596** Barents wintered in the Arctic
- **1724** Bering left for eastern Asia
- **1893-6** Nansen sailed across the Arctic
- **1909** Peary reached the North Pole

VITUS BERING

Bering served in the Russian Navy. In 1724 Peter the Great sent him to find out whether Asia was joined to North America. Bering discovered that the two continents were separated by a strait (narrow channel). It is now named after him – the Bering Strait.

WILLEM BARENTS

The Dutch sent Willem Barents to explore the areas to the north and east of Norway, where they believed they might find a northeast passage to the Pacific Ocean.

In 1596 Barents was sailing off the coast of Novaya Zemlya in the Arctic Ocean when the sea began to freeze over. Winter was beginning and the crew was trapped.

Ice formed round the ship, cracking its timbers and forcing it up out of the water. The sailors walked across the ice till they got to shore, carrying with them wood from the ship. They built a hut out of the wood and they stayed there all through the winter, on a shore that they named 'Ice Haven'. It was so cold that the wine froze in their glasses and the sheets froze on their beds. The men survived the winter by hunting animals and living off the supplies from the ship.

In 1871, nearly 300 years later, another expedition found the hut, just as Barents and his men had left it. The cooking pots and weapons, the ship's clock and even the cabin boy's boots, were still there, preserved by the cold.

PEOPLE OF THE ARCTIC

The Inuit were expert at surviving in the extreme cold. Their clothes were warmer and lighter than anything the explorers could make. They dressed in jackets and trousers of sealskin. Their boots were stuffed with moss. In winter they travelled by dog-sled and, when the thaw came, they used kayaks – canoes made of whale bone and hide.

53

THE EXPLORERS OF THE SOUTH POLE

The explorers who tried to reach the South Pole faced terrible dangers. Ships sailing around Antarctica met

icebergs big enough to sink them. To the south, the Ross Ice Shelf, a vast cliff of ice, bars the way to the Antarctic continent. The land at the South Pole is a mixture of snow-fields and mountain peaks. Hidden under the snow there are crevasses – deep cracks in the ice which can swallow up a sled or a team of dogs. Hunger, fatigue, cold and frostbite are all enemies of travellers in the Antarctic.

JAMES CLARK ROSS

An officer in the British navy, James Clark Ross was the first man to discover the North Magnetic Pole between 1829 and 1833.

He also explored the Antarctic: in 1841 he took two strong ships, the *Erebus* and the *Terror*, south through pack-ice and past live volcanoes until they came to a great wall of ice. This is now called the Ross Ice Shelf.

TWO POLES

There are two South Poles. One is the South Magnetic Pole. This is the point which draws the needle of the compass. The other is the geographic South Pole. This is in the exact centre of the Antarctic Circle and is the point that Scott and Amundsen were trying to reach. In the same way there are two North Poles.

SOUTH AMERICA

SOUTH ATLANTIC OCEAN

Weddell Sea

Ronne Ice Shelf

ANTARCTICA

South Pole

Ross Sea

Bay of Whales

Ross Ice Shelf

McMurdo Sound

South Magnetic Pole

SOUTH PACIFIC OCEAN

Antarctic Circle

RACE FOR THE SOUTH POLE

In 1911 two expeditions set out to reach the South Pole. One was British: Captain Robert Scott sailed from London in the *Terra Nova* towards Antarctica. He took with him a large team of scientists, including a film cameraman. When he reached Melbourne in Australia, he found a telegram waiting for him. It was from Roald Amundsen, a Norwegian explorer, who planned to race him to the Pole. Amundsen's team started the journey from his base in the Bay of Whales on 20th October 1911. They travelled quickly because they had little to carry. On 14th December 1911, they reached the South Pole, where they raised the Norwegian flag and put up a tent. Inside they left letters for Scott. Then they returned to their ship and sailed safely home.

Scott left from his base at McMurdo Sound on 1st November 1911, but the ponies that he planned to use in the final stretch to the Pole died in the extreme cold. Scott's men had to help pull the sledges themselves because Scott had not brought enough dogs. The expedition soon ran into trouble. The men grew very tired and Scott had to send back the sledges one after another, until there was only one left. On 18th January 1912, Scott and four team-mates reached the South Pole. There they found the Norwegian flag, so they knew that Amundsen had beaten them to it. They started to make their way back to base, but they were very tired and suffering badly from frostbite. Not one of them reached the base camp. All five died on the way.

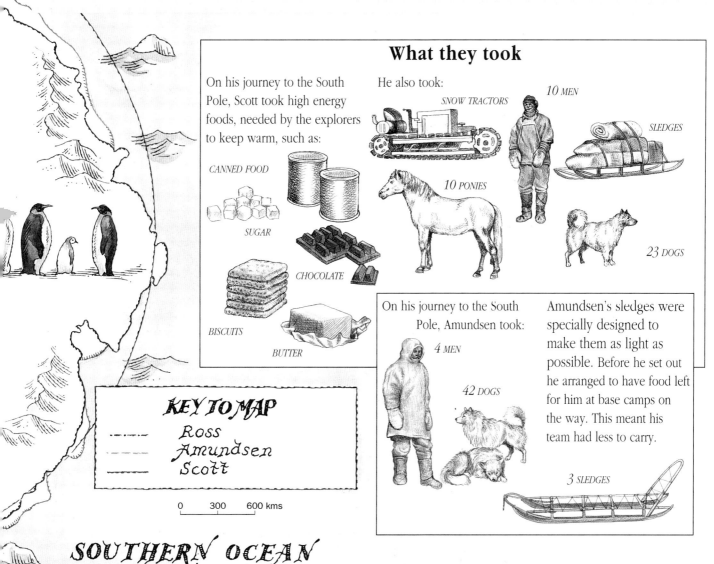

What they took

On his journey to the South Pole, Scott took high energy foods, needed by the explorers to keep warm, such as:

CANNED FOOD

SUGAR

CHOCOLATE

BISCUITS

BUTTER

He also took:

SNOW TRACTORS

10 PONIES

10 MEN

SLEDGES

23 DOGS

On his journey to the South Pole, Amundsen took:

4 MEN

42 DOGS

3 SLEDGES

Amundsen's sledges were specially designed to make them as light as possible. Before he set out he arranged to have food left for him at base camps on the way. This meant his team had less to carry.

KEY TO MAP
- · — · — Ross
- — — — Amundsen
- ——— Scott

0   300   600 kms

SOUTHERN OCEAN

OCEAN EXPLORATION

Deep down at the bottom of the ocean it is pitch dark and very cold. The pressure of the water becomes more and more intense the further you go down. We have only been able to explore the great depths of the oceans within the last 150 years or so as a result of the advance of technology.

The first undersea explorers were skin divers who hunted for pearls, sponges and corals. They could only stay down for as long as they could hold their breath. Then, about 400 years ago, people began to look for ways to go deeper and stay down longer. In 1624 Cornelius Drebbel, a Dutchman, built the first successful submarine. It was egg-shaped and made of wood. Twelve oarsmen rowed it along.

THE DIVING SUIT

In 1829 a German, Augustus Siebe, designed the diving-suit, which provided more freedom of movement. The boots were made of brass or lead and were very heavy, in order to stop the diver floating up to the surface.

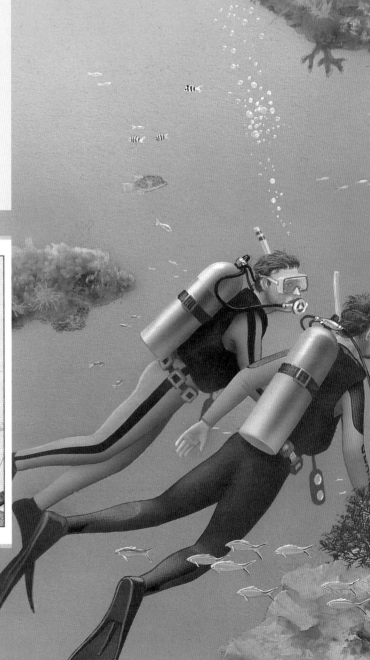

THE DIVING BELL

Another idea developed in the 16th century was the diving bell. This was a metal waterproof container filled with air. The diver went into it and was lowered to the bottom of the sea, where he stayed until the air in the bell was used up.

In the early 18th century, Edmund Halley invented a way of changing the air supply inside the bell by lowering barrels of fresh air down to it.

HMS CHALLENGER

The first ship equipped for ocean exploration, *HMS Challenger,* set out in 1872 to explore and measure the Pacific, Atlantic and Indian Oceans. The scientists found that the sea bed has mountains, valleys and even underwater volcanoes, and that life exists deep below the ocean's surface. They measured the deepest sea in the world, the Mariana Trench in the Pacific, where the ocean floor is more than 11,000 metres deep.

THE BATHYSPHERE AND BATHYSCAPHE

In 1930 Otis Barton and William Beebe invented the bathysphere, a steel ball with portholes of quartz. Inside this the men reached a depth of 906 metres, the deepest that anyone had yet reached.

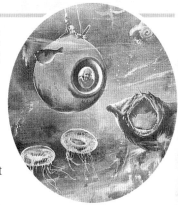

The bathyscaphe or 'deep boat', was invented by Auguste Piccard. In 1960 it touched an incredible depth of 10,916 metres. Piccard's son, Jacques, and Don Walsh, the two men inside, found that creatures and plants lived even at this depth.

THE AQUALUNG

The aqualung was invented in 1943 by the French underwater explorer, Jacques-Yves Cousteau, and by an engineer, Emile Gagnan. It allowed divers to swim to depths of up to 30 metres without being attached to a ship. This is because they carried their own air supply with them in a cylinder fastened to their back. A tube took the air from the cylinder to the diver's mouth.

THE DANGERS OF OCEAN EXPLORATION

Deep-sea diving has long been dangerous because of a condition known as 'the bends', which can cripple or kill a diver. This happens when a diver comes up to the surface too quickly, so that bubbles of nitrogen form in the blood. Although we know how to prevent it, divers are still at risk from the bends, as well as from problems brought about by heat loss and from 'rapture of the deep' – a condition sometimes caused by breathing nitrogen under pressure. This causes a type of drunkenness.

One way of avoiding these problems is to use robots. These can be sent down a long way to gather samples and to take photographs. They are also used to repair oil pipelines. Another way is to build a saturation habitat (an underwater station) for the divers. These have been constructed underwater at depths of up to 180 metres and they are crewed by divers living there for days or weeks at a time.

SPACE EXPLORATION

Throughout history people have been fascinated by the mystery of what lies beyond our planet. Limited to watching and calculating from Earth, we have been unable, until the second half of the 20th century, to explore for ourselves the vast unknown expanse of space.

Born in 1473, the Polish astronomer Copernicus (shown left) was the first person to explain that the planets move around the Sun. Galileo, an Italian born in 1564, invented a telescope used to discover Jupiter's satellites and the craters on the Moon.

As telescopes became more sophisticated, astronomers discovered more about different planets and solar systems. Pluto, at the furthest edge of our solar system, was named in 1930. Astronomers saw huge dying stars called supernovas, which shone out very brightly then disappeared. However, telescopes showed astronomers only a limited amount. To learn more about space, they needed to travel in space. A German, Wernher von Braun, designed the first working rocket, called the *V-2*. These were used by the Germans in World War 2. After the war, von Braun helped the Americans build space rockets. The first American rockets reached a height of 112 kilometres.

PEOPLE IN SPACE

In 1957 the Russians launched the first man-made satellite. A satellite is an object which

orbits (goes round) a planet. In the same year they sent up another satellite, this time containing a dog: Laika was the first living creature to travel in space. In 1961 the Russians sent the first man into space. His name was Yuri Gagarin. He orbited the Earth once before making a safe landing 108 minutes later.

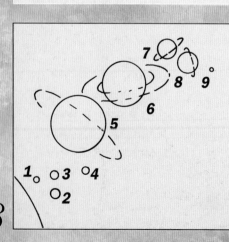

Distance of planets from the Sun

	Planet	Distance
1	Mercury:	57,900,000 kms
2	Venus:	108,200,000 kms
3	Earth:	149,600,000 kms
4	Mars:	227,900,000 kms
5	Jupiter:	778,300,000 kms
6	Saturn:	1,427,000,000 kms
7	Uranus:	2,869,600,000 kms
8	Neptune:	4,496,700,000 kms
9	Pluto:	5,900,000,000 kms

. . . AND ON THE MOON

By the early 1960s, it was a race between the Americans and the Russians to put the first man on the Moon. The Americans were first in 1969. All over the world, millions watched as Neil Armstrong and Buzz Aldrin stepped out of the *Apollo 11* space capsule onto the surface of the Moon. Neil Armstrong called it 'one small step for man, a giant leap for mankind.'

After this, there were five more landings on the Moon, and astronauts brought back rock samples. Scientists studying them have learned much about the Moon's age and make-up.

BEYOND THE MOON

In 1977 the Americans sent out two probes to explore the solar system and beyond: *Voyager 1* and *Voyager 2* both headed for Jupiter and Saturn. *Voyager 1* then headed out of the solar system; *Voyager 2* was programmed to travel on past Uranus and Neptune, taking pictures as it went. The distance between the outer planets is enormous: it took *Voyager 2* five years to travel from Saturn to Uranus and another three years to travel to Neptune. The pictures taken by *Voyager 2* from millions of kilometres away showed us things which no one had ever seen before: volcanoes on Jupiter's moon Io, storms on Saturn, and icy geysers on Triton, one of Saturn's moons.

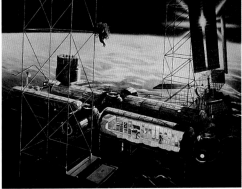

If people are to reach these distant planets, they will have to stay in space for a very long time. In 1986 the Russians set up the space station Mir, where astronauts live for several months, as part of an experiment to find out how long people can safely stay in space. The USA, Russia, Europe, Canada and Japan are currently collaborating on a space station, the ISS (International Space Station), due for completion in about 2005. Later, a manned landing on Mars may be the next great step in space exploration.

THE FUTURE OF EXPLORATION

We have now explored almost all of the Earth's surface. Because of this, modern-day exploration has come to be something quite different from what it was in previous centuries. Gone are the days when courageous men and women set out for unexplored territories, not knowing whether they would survive the hazards of hostile tribes, unknown diseases or wild animals. Explorers of recent times still have uncharted territories on Earth to explore, such as the densest parts of the rainforest, the Antarctic regions and the oceans. But for the main part, the 'explorers' of the 20th century are scientists and conservationists, eager to learn about the Earth and its climate, the balance that exists between all of the Earth's living things and ways to preserve and protect this balance.

THE ANTARCTIC

This was the last area on Earth to be fully explored when, in 1958, an expedition crossed the continent of Antarctica for the first time. There are still large areas of this freezing continent that are not known to us in any detail, but this is gradually changing as there are many international scientific stations based here. Scientists study the layers of ice, which show the composition of the snow that has fallen here over the last 160,000 years, and from this they can find out about long-term changes in the climate and atmosphere.

THE RAINFORESTS

The tropical rainforests of Africa and South America contain millions of different animal and plant species, most of which have not been identified or named. In the more remote areas, there is still a lot of scientific exploration that can be done, especially with regard to the 'canopy' of the rainforest (this is the name given to the mass of foliage high up in the trees).

Exploration has been damaging to the rainforests as it has led to people living outside the area destroying the rainforest for their own profit, by activities such as tree-felling, mining and cattle-grazing. Now institutions such as the Royal Geographical Society, which has sponsored exploration since the 1830s, send scientists to study the plants and animals of the forest in an effort to reverse the damage that has been caused.

STILL UNEXPLORED

Other areas that have been only partly explored include high mountainous areas, underground rivers and caves (see left), the ocean bed and desert areas. Scientific projects continue to bring to light new facts on the Earth's make-up and to monitor the changes that are taking place all the time, such as the expansion of the desert regions.

THE SKY IS THE LIMIT

The biggest single challenge for people as explorers is that of space. In the years since 1957, when the first space satellite was launched by the Russians, space travel has advanced in leaps and bounds. It is possible that the 21st century will see someone stepping on to the planet Mars. However, space is endless and unknown. We cannot foresee a time when people have explored the vast wonder of space.

INDEX

ACKNOWLEDGEMENTS

Senior designer: Susi Martin
Designers: Jane Warring, Brazzle Atkins
Editor: Sarah Allen
Picture Researchers: Lorraine Sennett, Liz Heasman

Illustrators: John Woodcock (Spectron Artists): main maps; Tony Lodge (Spectron Artists): inset maps; Kevin Jones Associates: pp22-23, pp56-57 & pp58-59; Lindi Norton: pp4-5; Bob Venables (Spectron Artists): all other artwork.

Photographs: Ancient Art & Architecture: 29; Bibliothèque Nationale: 12-13, 15; Bodleian Library, MS.Bodl.264, fol.259v: 16; Bridgeman Art Library: 3, 27, 34, 35, 53; Bruce Coleman: 2, 38; Dagli Orti: 18, 19, 20, 24, 28; Mary Evans Picture Library: 3, 9, 11, 12, 16, 20, 22, 34, 40, 44, 45, 46, 48, 51, 52, 54, 56, 57; Michael Holford: 6, 7; Chris Howes: 61; Hulton Deutsch Collection: 30; David Keith Jones/Images of Africa Photobank: 49; Mansell Collection: 24; Natural History Museum: 3, 37; National Maritime Museum: 41; Royal Geographical Society: 33, 61; Royal Geographical Society, London/Bridgeman Art Library: 8, 36, 38, 43, 48; Science Photo Library: 58, 59, 60, 61; Werner Forman Archive: 3.

Every effort has been made to contact the holders of copyright material, but if any have been inadvertently overlooked, the publishers will be pleased to make any necessary amendments.

© 1993 HarperCollins*Publishers* Ltd
First published in 1993. Reprinted 1999

ISBN 000 198358 X

Printed in Great Britain by Scotprint Ltd, Musselburgh